ESCAPE OR DIE

AN ESCAPE ARTIST UNLOCKS
THE SECRET TO CHEATING DEATH

ANTHONY MARTIN

Escape or Die: An escape artist unlocks the secret to cheating death

Published by:
Genesis Publishing Group
2002 Skyline Place
Bartlesville, OK 74006
www.genesis-group.net

© 2013 Anthony Martin. All rights reserved. No part of this publication may be reproduced, stored in a retrieval system, or transmitted by any means—electronic, mechanical, photographic (photocopying), recording, or otherwise—without prior permission in writing.

Edited by Lynn Copeland

Printed in the United States of America

ISBN 978-1-933591-13-1

Unless otherwise indicated, Scripture quotations are from the *New King James Version*, © 1979, 1980, 1982 by Thomas Nelson Inc., Publishers, Nashville, Tennessee.

Scripture quotations marked "NIV1984" taken from the HOLY BIBLE, NEW INTERNATIONAL VERSION®. Copyright © 1973, 1978, 1984 Biblica. Used by permission of Zondervan. All rights reserved.

CONTENTS

FOREWORD, *by Ray Comfort* 5

INTRODUCTION 7

CHAPTER 1   Christmas Gifts and Ripcords 11

CHAPTER 2   Houdini, Spirits, and Psychics 19

CHAPTER 3   Assessing Ourselves .31

CHAPTER 4   The Man in the Box .41

CHAPTER 5   Truth or Consequences 55

CHAPTER 6   One Way Out 63

CHAPTER 7   The Perfect Parachute 73

CHAPTER 8   Tracking 85

CHAPTER 9   Doing the Impossible 113

CAREER HIGHLIGHTS 131

Foreword

Gravity is a dog's best friend. I came to that conclusion after years of watching my dog follow my grandchildren around, as they clutched cookies in their tiny, sticky hands. His eyes would eagerly watch their every move as they stuffed the cookies into their mouths. Predictably half the delectable would succumb to the effects of gravity, much to the delight of my dog, who, incidentally, forever acts as though he's never been fed in his life.

Unlike Sam, I don't like gravity. I makes me nervous. This is because when I was seven years old I began climbing up a cliff and became paralyzed with fear when I was only about 20 feet off the ground. I could almost feel the pull of some invisible force beckoning to me to give myself to its power. It was a horrible feeling and one I get waves of with the occasional nightmare, or if I'm tempted to go near the edge of a high cliff. One of my uncles had to climb up and guide me down to safety.

Ironically, I don't mind floating 35,000 feet above the earth in a large tin can with wings. That's different. But if you think you could ever get me to jump from a plane—even with a perfectly packed parachute—please know that you would have infinitely more chance of flossing the back teeth of hungry lions at the L.A. Zoo at feeding time. It's not going to happen.

ESCAPE OR DIE

My good friend Anthony Martin jumps out of airplanes handcuffed. While on his way down (at 180 mph), he finds time to pick the locks and release the cuffs before floating to the ground and going home for lunch. The man is crazy. I've hinted that he should retire and play with snakes or something that sane people do. But he takes no notice. Probably because he didn't have any traumatic experiences as a normal kid that put some sense into him. Perhaps he was never told about gravity. Despite my horror at what he does, I admire him for his courage and am so pleased he has written this book.

The great Houdini still holds a sense of fascination for millions around the world. He was an amazing entertainer. But Tony Martin is different from the many imitators of Houdini. He's a man who seeks more than applause from an appreciative world. He has something to say that really is a matter of life and death. That's what this book is about. Hold on to each page with a special attentiveness as he takes you by the hand and gives you the keys to life's ultimate escape. *Escape or Die* isn't just a book title. It's the ultimate decree.

RAY COMFORT
Founder, LivingWaters.com

INTRODUCTION

> "No one wants to die. Even people who want to
> go to heaven don't want to die to get there.
> And yet death is the destination we all share.
> No one has ever escaped it."
> —STEVE JOBS, 2005 COMMENCEMENT ADDRESS
> AT STANFORD UNIVERSITY

I have been an escape artist my whole life. When I started at around age six, my hands slipped out of most handcuffs. As a child I grew up reading Superman and Captain Marvel comic books and dreaming that I could fly. Now as a trained skydiver, I sometimes feel I've achieved that childhood dream—but though it can feel like I'm flying, I still know the reality that I'm falling. I'm very aware that unlike my childhood heroes I'm not invincible, and that skydiving jumps, like most of my escapes, carry some possibility of harm.

As a risk taker by profession, it's my job to weigh risk versus reward and then prepare in such a way that the odds are always in my favor. But the fact is, no matter how careful I try to be, accidents still can happen and circumstances can be miscalculated. Over the years I have developed various ways to deal with those unexpected circumstances.

ESCAPE OR DIE

When I make the choice to jump out of an airplane, however, it is an irreversible decision. Once my body leaves the aircraft, I cannot change my mind and get back in. Within the first ten seconds I am already a thousand feet away. In the same way, when we leave this life through the door of death, it will be too late to make any decisions about our destiny. Our fate at that point has been irrevocably sealed.

You may never jump out of an airplane, yet we share a universal enemy. We all have one thing in common: everyone reading these pages will someday die. In fact, our demise is so certain that it's been said that health is merely the slowest possible way to achieve it. Death is one appointment that ultimately even the best of procrastinators must keep.

The clock is ticking... and we are running out of time.

The awareness of our own mortality has driven many of us to go to great lengths to leave some enduring mark. The Egyptian Pharaohs built pyramids to this end, and, not unlike them, we often attempt to build business empires or seek earthly prominence in the hopes of leaving some record of our existence for posterity. As an escape artist, over the years I have amassed a lengthy résumé of record-breaking escapes and stunts. Yet in retrospect, they are of no lasting value and have little importance when weighed in the scales of eternity. It would seem that although we recognize our own transience, we have thought much of preserving our memories and little of preserving ourselves.

Death is our common destiny—but is there something we can do to defeat it? Is it possible to actually escape this great enemy of humanity? These are some of the questions we will be exploring in this book. My purpose in addressing serious spiritual issues is to inspire in you a genuine and

Introduction

open-minded quest for real answers. This is one subject we cannot afford to be wrong about.

The book of Psalms says, "So teach us to number our days, that we may gain a heart of wisdom" (Psalm 90:12). Wisdom is defined as the right application of knowledge. We wouldn't seek knowledge about the hereafter unless we recognized our mortality or "numbered our days." Although you will leave your body at death, that won't be the end of you. Your soul—the real you that's looking out those "windows" we call eyes—will continue to exist somewhere for all eternity (Matthew 25:46). Our choices about the hereafter have eternal consequences. What choices have you made? Where will you go when you die? How can you know for sure?

Having risked death numerous times, I'd like to share my escape experiences with you as we consider these all-important questions. In these pages I will help you to weigh the risk versus reward for your own death-defying escape, and then prepare in such a way that you not only have the odds in your favor, but you can actually be assured of landing safely on the other side of this life.

Join me as we unlock the mystery of life after death and discover how to make the greatest escape of all.

CHAPTER 1

CHRISTMAS GIFTS AND RIPCORDS

"Truth is so obscure in these times, and falsehood so established, that unless we love the truth, we cannot know it."

—BLAISE PASCAL

My journey as an escape artist began on Christmas 1972 in the Midwestern home of my Grandma and Grandpa Huber. The whole family—cousins, aunts, and uncles—would gather there every year for Christmas. My grandma always had the best Christmas tree, and I remember the pride I felt in helping to set up the tree and hang the ornaments. The ornaments were antiques and I always liked the sense of history that such things conveyed to me. In the mid-1970s magician Doug Henning would have his annual television special this time of year, and together our family would watch in amazement as this engaging Canadian would defy all known natural laws, much to my delight.

It was at one of these gatherings that I received a gift that would forever send me on my life's journey. I don't recall opening the box but I do remember seeing my

ESCAPE OR DIE

first inexplicable miracle in person. My father was levitating a magic wand underneath his hand with no apparent means of support. Now, I knew he was no more a magician than I was, yet the contents of this box empowered him to do the seemingly impossible. I was mesmerized and awestruck—I too must have this power. After all, if he could do it so quickly, it must be magic.

It was then that he tilted his hand and the balloon burst. The left hand that was grasping his right wrist during the levitation had its index finger pointing straight out, holding the "magic" wand. I kicked myself for not noticing the missing finger of his left hand during the trick. Somehow things changed for me at that moment; the wonder that the unexplained had caused was shattered. There was no Santa Claus, no Easter Bunny, and now, no magic. Doug Henning's specials were never the same after that. My eyes had been opened and I could now see the strings on every puppet and the birds up every sleeve. It was all smoke and mirrors, and from that moment forward I was a little wiser and not a little disappointed that there was no real magic.

Finding Truth

It was later that same evening that my hope revived when I discovered a small lock and chain inside the magic set. The chain resembled a dog choker or leash and came with instructions on how one could be fastened in it yet escape. My interest was sparked again—could there still be real magic? I hoped that there could be. I threw the instructions aside and examined the chain and lock very carefully searching for a gimmick. I could find none. When all else failed, as a last resort I went back to the instructions (my, how we males hate to do that). The instructions explained a technique that could be used to retain slack while being

Christmas Gifts and Ripcords

chained, enabling one to escape. This, at last, could resolve my disappointments. Skill and knowledge could be used to do real escapes. This was as close to real "magic" as a person could get.

Over the next several months, my older cousin Tom and I began putting on small performances for the family. I would have my wrists chained and then be placed into a trunk from which I would successfully escape. The obligatory smattering of applause was enough to encourage me, and to my parents' chagrin, I was hooked. In the following years, while other children would ask their grandparents for candy at the department store, I would ask my grandpa to purchase locks. In my quest for knowledge I would take the locks apart to try to discover how they worked. I was to spend many nights burning the midnight oil learning the secrets that the little mechanisms would, after much effort, reluctantly divulge. As my classmates participated in school events and sporting activities, my time was spent in my crude basement laboratory with locks and handcuffs. My grandma's bathroom door still stands as a testimony to my learning curve: to this day it no longer locks. At times, I guess, I opened the locks too well. I shaped pieces of wire

Anthony "The Handcuff King" (age 10)

ESCAPE OR DIE

First paid show at the Kiel Picnic, 1976
(Note the mother's touch: a turban, for an air of mystery.)

that could open the locks and felt the satisfaction of possessing knowledge (and therefore power) that others did not. Later in life I was to establish friendships with registered locksmiths and was able to learn the more traditional methods used to compromise locks. Yet, it was those very early years that produced the effective, albeit unorthodox, methods that I still employ today.

These experiences cemented my disdain for the false and admiration for all that is real. My first police-substantiated escape was at our local county jail when I was just thirteen years old. The local sheriff searched, handcuffed, and even straitjacketed me and I, of course, was able to get free. That first official escape landed me on the front page of our local newspaper.

Of all the escapes of my career, however, the path to my greatest escape began when I was a young boy. I remember hearing a passage from the Bible: "you do not know what will happen tomorrow. For what is your life? It is even a vapor that appears for a little time and then vanishes away" (James 4:14). Even as a boy, I knew that this life doesn't last forever. We may not even make it to tomorrow. So I began a search for the solution—and found the key to everlasting life, the way to escape from death itself.

What had begun as a disappointment that Christmas day had sent me on an exploratory journey for the truth. I found that real escapes need not be a con but could be based on knowledge and acquired skills. Spiritual journeys are like this as well. To find the answers you must earnestly look for them. You must seek them with a sense of urgency.

He Who Hesitates Is Lost

Some time ago I was visiting a skydiving drop zone in my native Wisconsin and saw that the skydivers there were making parachute jumps from a DC3. The DC3 is a fixed-wing, propeller-driven aircraft that was a competitor of the Boeing 247. I had never jumped from a DC3 and naturally was eager to do it. I didn't have my own parachute along but was "fortunate" enough to be able to borrow an extra one from a friend at the drop zone. Parachute in hand, I purchased my jump ticket and waited patiently to get on the mammoth bird. Before long, the plane was full of jumpers and we were taking to the sky for another freefall adventure.

Jump altitude was announced and the plane door was quickly opened. The view of the earth was obscured by the clouds that were now far beneath us. Several skydivers jumped before me so I waited a few seconds to allow some horizontal separation and then leaped for those clouds I had admired just moments before. I did some basic maneuvers—front loops, back loops, and barrel rolls—before reaching for the ripcord. To my horror the ripcord

ESCAPE OR DIE

was gone! I felt for the handle and it was missing. Looking over my shoulder I could see the handle flapping around behind me still attached to the strap that pulls the pin. I frantically grabbed for it as it mocked me just outside my reach. After several more attempts to no avail, I made the ultimate decision: I pulled my reserve chute.

When my reserve opened I was only about 100 feet from the ground. I was shocked to see how close I had been to death. A truck from across the nearby highway sped to the field where I landed to see what had become of me. Their faces told the story when they saw me standing there unscathed. It was as if they saw a ghost. They said they saw me fall behind the trees and never did see a parachute open. They were expecting to find a crumpled body, but found a miracle instead: I was still alive! That's how close I was.

> *I did some basic maneuvers before reaching for the ripcord. To my horror the ripcord was gone!*

I should have pulled my reserve immediately after seeing the danger I was in. Hesitation almost cost me my life. Hesitation can likewise cost you your soul.

The famous musician and former Beatle John Lennon, when asked about his future plans, was quoted in December 1980 as saying, "There's plenty of time, right? Plenty of time." Two days later a deranged fan shot and killed Lennon on the steps of his New York apartment building. For John Lennon, there simply wasn't "plenty of time"—and the same is true for us. We never know which day will be our last.

Beloved President John F. Kennedy (who also was tragically killed by an assassin's bullet) is quoted as saying, "There are risks and costs to action. But they are far less

Christmas Gifts and Ripcords

than the long-range risks of comfortable inaction." As a skydiver and an escape artist, nothing is surer to take your life than hesitation. The moment that you realize you are in danger, you must act. Anything less is to contribute to your own ruin.

It is my prayer that you'll be too concerned about your soul to hesitate and will want immediate answers to this ancient mystery of life after death. This will require a measure of inner honesty and openness. Being honest with ourselves in assessing our own strengths and weaknesses is a requisite trait for an escape artist. This ability has saved my life on countless occasions. It is also necessary when evaluating our spiritual condition. Such inner sincerity leads us to put pride aside and desire the truth no matter how ugly or humbling it is. It is a trait that absolutely needs to be timely in its application. As can be seen by my jump from the DC3, there are decisions in life that are too important to ignore or waver about. Albert Einstein is quoted as saying, "The right to search for the truth implies also a duty; one must not conceal any part of what one has recognized to be the truth."

I have found the most difficult truths to discover aren't the ones people conceal from us. They are the ones hidden by our own pride and feelings of self-sufficiency.

CHAPTER 2

HOUDINI, SPIRITS, AND PSYCHICS

"It is dangerous to let the public behind the scenes. They are easily disillusioned and then they are angry with you, for it was the illusion they loved."
—WILLIAM SOMERSET MAUGHAM

The only light came from a flickering candle flame whose shadow danced ominously on the wall. Eight people sat clutching hands around the table in the tiny room. The atmosphere seemed more like a wake than a quest for answers. Scattered on the table were a bell, a tambourine, and a brass horn. The group anxiously exchanged glances as the candle was blown out. Now there was only darkness—a darkness so oppressive it could be felt.

The seekers shuddered in the room turned gateway—an entrance into what they hoped would be the supernatural. Suddenly, the bell was heard to ring with no apparent operator. The horn appeared luminous in the darkness, floating high above the now petrified onlookers. Then the voice, a deep monotone, addressed the group.

"Whom do you seek...what do you want from us... why do you disturb our rest?"

ESCAPE OR DIE

An elderly woman in the group began to shake and sob. "Our son Thomas," she replied. "I must hear from Thomas."

Vaudeville legend Harry Houdini spent the last years of his life involved in dramatic scenes such as this. He too was a seeker, but he found only parlor tricks and chicanery wherever he went. Houdini was looking in all the wrong places for the answers to what happens after death.

Fakes, Frauds, and Counterfeits

According to a 2009 CBS News poll, it is estimated that over half of Americans believe in psychic phenomenon. Among this group are those who take these beliefs a step further and seek personal guidance by such means. After the death of Houdini's mother in 1913, he was to undertake a journey into a labyrinth filled with fraud and deceit. At that time it was not uncommon to seek the aid of "spirit mediums" who claimed to be able to speak to the spirits of dearly departed loved ones. The First World War had snatched thousands into eternity and people had become desperate to communicate with those they had lost. When Houdini attempted to contact his beloved mother on the other side and found empty trickery instead, he took matters personally. He went on a crusade to expose such charlatans and stop their attempts to prey on a gullible, unsuspecting public.

Although such séances still take place today, the majority of those seeking guidance from beyond turn to people who profess to have psychic abilities. A glance at the Yellow Pages will reveal that the practice continues unabated, and it has become quite lucrative for those who engage in it. Astrology, horoscopes, and psychic readings have captured the imagination of a public that is searching for answers. In 2011, Florida prosecutors, who were cooperating in a multi-state investigation, say a fortune-telling scam amassed

Houdini, Spirits, and Psychics

over $30 million for its practitioners. Those scammed forked over cash, gold, and jewelry in an attempt to receive supernatural guidance and comfort. Even the U.S. government managed to spend an amazing $20 million over several decades (beginning in the 1970s) in a vain attempt to gather intelligence from psychics before coming to its senses.

In an effort to refute such practices, I developed an act that duplicates much of this phenomenon that many people so readily put their trust in. In the act, I appear to know things I couldn't possibly know and see things I couldn't possibly see, which challenges the audience to question the validity of such belief systems.

There is, however, a paradox in all of this. It is difficult to reconcile how people can be thoroughly gullible in one area while at the same time being very skeptical and investigative in others. The answer may lie in what we want to believe. As a locksmith and escape artist, I've found that fakes, frauds, and counterfeits have extended far beyond the realm of just spirit mediums and psychics. They extend right into my own profession.

Some People Follow Illusions

Like a hammer to a carpenter or a brush to a painter, a straitjacket is a basic tool of the trade to an escape artist. To perform a straitjacket escape today is by no means original. The straitjacket escape was done in full view of the audience for the very first time by Houdini's brother, Hardeen, in 1905. Prior to this, Houdini had always done the escape behind a curtained enclosure so that his methods would remain mysterious. It was Hardeen who discovered that the struggle was good theater and pioneered the full-view straitjacket escape that we are familiar with today. Houdini was later to adopt this practice himself, further improving

ESCAPE OR DIE

on it by being suspended upside down from the ankles high over the heads of onlookers.

Over the years, I've performed the straitjacket escape under every circumstance imaginable, including my 25th Anniversary Jail Cell Escape (from the Waushara County Jail) for Ripley's Believe It or Not! For that escape I was laced in a straitjacket and, as an added obstacle, strapped to a ladder before being locked behind four prison doors. The Waushara County Jail in Wisconsin, at one time known for housing Edward Gein, "America's Most Bizarre Murderer," was able to hold me for just under three minutes.

Strapped to a ladder at the Waushara County Jail

Most people today don't realize that the majority of straitjacket escapes they've seen were not genuine. Instead, the straitjackets were cleverly faked. I perform escapes using only real straitjackets and have been harshly criticized for revealing on national television how fake straitjackets work. People who use trick handcuffs and straitjackets are really the equivalent of actors who pretend to be singers and lip synch their songs. Television has further perpetuated the falsehood with audience plants, clever camera angles, and deceptive video editing techniques. Such mimicry cheats audiences, as well as cheapens the risk in-

Houdini, Spirits, and Psychics

volved in the real thing. Imagine the humiliation of failing an escape attempt, or even worse, getting killed because the zipper got stuck on your fake straitjacket.

One thing I have noticed about the fake jackets is that they have more straps, making them look better to audiences—more secure, more menacing. Like the airbrushed photo of your favorite celebrity, they look almost perfect. When placed side-by-side with the real thing, however, subtle differences are apparent. The arm holes are larger in the fake jacket. The arm-retaining strap exits from inside the jacket instead of being attached to the outside. The material is thinner and more supple, among other telltale clues. Just like the methods used to identify counterfeit money, when the fake jacket is placed next to the real thing, the truth is told.

Before his death on Halloween in 1926, Houdini made a pact with his wife to attempt to communicate with her from beyond the grave. In his mind, this final test under his direction would conclusively reveal whether spirit communication was possible and, more importantly, reveal what's on the other side of death. Despite repeated failures, Houdini's wife faithfully followed his instructions and held séances every year thereafter. On October 31, 1936, Bess Houdini held the last Houdini séance. There, on the roof of the Knickerbocker Hotel in Hollywood, she announced that she would stop all further efforts to contact her deceased husband. This decision finally brought to an end a full ten years of attempted spirit communication with the late magician. Unfortunately, some people never stop wasting their lives dealing with the disappointments of fakes, frauds, and counterfeits when it comes to spiritual beliefs.

I've developed an escape called the "Cangue Crypt" (a scaled-down version of the "Buried Alive: Crystal

ESCAPE OR DIE

Crypt" escape described later). A cangue is an ancient Chinese instrument similar to the western pillory. It's a large, flat board with a hole cut in the center big enough for a person's neck. This challenge requires me to kneel while my hands are handcuffed behind my back. A hood is draped over my head, and the cangue is locked around my neck. Finally, a clear plastic box is placed over my head so that it rests on the cangue. The box, containing my head, is then filled with about twenty pounds of sand. I need to escape from the handcuffs in order to release myself so I can breathe again. This escape is indeed dangerous and conjures many fears in the minds of those watching (not to mention in my own).

Some people, it would seem, live their whole lives in a cangue. As the sands of time march on, they are edging ever closer to their own inevitable crypt. All they need is the key that can set them free and give them the breath of life. They are trapped and tragically unaware of the consequences.

Our pluralistic society has caused confusion by presenting many religious ideas as truths, even though these "truths" are not compatible and often contradict each other. Television celebrities, philosophers, authors, and religious gurus peddle varying views of eternity—all of which cannot be true. One view points to a god that is nonjudgmental where anything goes, while another points to a god that must be appeased by the good deeds that we do. One religion will teach that god is personal, another that god is an unknowable force. Some speak of an eternal paradise that we must work to merit, while others have their adherents strive through reincarnation to reach a point where their souls are absorbed and they cease individual consciousness. The Bible cautions us, "Beloved, do not believe every spirit, but test the spirits, whether they are of God; because

Houdini, Spirits, and Psychics

many false prophets have gone out into the world" (1 John 4:1). We would do well to heed this advice and test religious teachings (spirits) to see if they are true. Truth will always withstand testing.

In many religions, people are deemed to be members just because of their culture or the family they were born into. They may participate in religious practices out of respect for their parents, or social custom, or simply because it has become a habit or tradition. Most people are very sincere and genuinely believe what they were taught. Ultimately, we are all responsible to take the time to put our beliefs to the test and investigate whether what we believe is true. Lies can be the most secure of prisons.

> *Ultimately, we are all responsible to take the time to put our beliefs to the test and investigate whether what we believe is true.*

I heard a story regarding one of Houdini's jail escapes. He was in Scotland, as the story goes, getting ready for a performance at one of the theaters. In an effort to advertise the show, he had himself handcuffed and locked in a cell at the local police station. The police officials and a modest ensemble of local reporters retired to a separate part of the building to await the Great Houdini's escape. Harry got the handcuffs off with little trouble but was struggling with the lock on the jail cell door. He used all the skill he could muster, yet the jail cell lock would not budge. Thinking he was finally defeated and forever embarrassed, in exhaustion he leaned against the cell door. The door swung open of its own accord. The jailer had neglected to lock the door!

Locks can be designed to keep people in prison or they can be designed to keep us safe. As truth seekers, we need to test the security of our beliefs. We need to make sure that we are not bound in the prison of a lie but are safe in the security of tested truth.

The Escape Plan

Every escape I have ever done began with an examination of the challenge and then the formulation of an escape plan. For the rest of our literary visit I will often refer to the Bible in discussing our plan to escape from death itself. In the advertisements for Houdini's 1926 Spirit Exposé tour there are some interesting caveats mentioned. One of them plainly states, "At no time will Houdini discuss the Bible or biblical quotations." We can only speculate as to why he felt the need to avoid discussing Scripture. I, on the other hand, cannot present the Truth to you without it.

Just as I went to the instructions as a last resort for the chain escape, we often try everything else first before humbling ourselves and seeking God for the answers. Many excellent books have been written that attest to the authority and reliability of the Bible as the Word of God, so it would be silly for me to try to cover ground that others have covered so well. The fact of the matter is, the Bible is not just a book. It's actually sixty-six books written over a span of about 1,500 years. It's unique in continuity in that the men God inspired to record it never contradict each other, despite the fact that it has over forty authors. The Bible's historical record is infallible and archaeology has yet to dispute one fact of any biblical accounts. In fact, there have been more than 25,000 archaeological finds proving that the people, places, and events mentioned in the Bible are real and are accurately described.

With over 24,000 ancient portions of the New Testament in existence, there is more manuscript evidence for

Houdini, Spirits, and Psychics

the Bible than for any ten pieces of classical literature combined, and the Dead Sea Scrolls discovered in 1949 prove that the Scriptures have not changed down through the ages, as some claim. In addition, its prophecies have no equal. Unlike other religious texts, the Bible contains thousands of detailed prophecies and records their precise fulfillment. They tell of the rise and fall of empires and leaders, as well as national calamities—all with 100 percent accuracy. It's estimated that more than a fourth of the Bible is predictive prophecy, proving it is the inspired Word of God, the only One who knows the future. Forty-seven copies of this extraordinary Book are sold or distributed throughout the world every minute of every day. Although each religion has texts that it claims are authoritative, they are either the teachings of men compiled by men, or have supposedly been dictated by angels. Only the Bible claims to be the Word of God, written by God Himself.

British preacher Charles Spurgeon is quoted as saying, "Defend the Bible? I would just as soon defend a lion. Just turn the Bible loose. It will defend itself." I tend to agree with him.

This extraordinary Book, the Word of God, makes it very clear that there is only one God: "I am the Lord, and there is no other; there is no God besides Me" (Isaiah 45:5). We are not in a position to go "god shopping" to find the one we like best. There is only one true God, the Creator of Heaven and earth.

The good news is, God is not hiding from us. There is a clear teaching that runs throughout Scripture that anyone who honestly seeks God can find Him (John 7:17). God Himself confirms this truth by stating, "And you will seek Me and find Me, when you search for Me with all your heart" (Jeremiah 29:13). Even nature itself, through its incredible order, design, and complexity, declares the existence of God (Romans 1:20).

Scripture tells us that there is only one God, yet He has revealed Himself as the Father, the Son, and the Holy Spirit. This concept of a "Triune" God, or Trinity, may be the most difficult attribute of God to grasp, yet Scripture repeatedly teaches it. First John 5:7 says, "For there are three that bear witness in heaven: the Father, the Word [Jesus Christ], and the Holy Spirit; and these three are one."

God has no beginning or end and He never changes (Malachi 3:6). He is eternal, and dwells outside the dimension of time, which He created. Genesis, the first book of the Bible, starts by saying, "In the beginning God…" He is described as having limitless power and control over the universe. He spoke creation into existence and all things are carefully maintained by His omnipotent hand.

God is Spirit (John 4:24), and as such He is not limited by space. He is present everywhere at the same time (Jeremiah 23:23,24). He is also all-knowing; there is nothing outside His knowledge. God is incapable of being surprised or caught off-guard. The Bible says, "You comprehend my path and my lying down, and are acquainted with all my ways. For there is not a word on my tongue, but behold, O Lord, You know it altogether" (Psalm 139:3,4).

The Scriptures describe God as being, "Holy, holy, holy" (Isaiah 6:3), the only characteristic of God emphasized three consecutive times. When we speak of God's holiness we speak of His divinity, purity, righteousness, and the fact that He is morally and ethically perfect. There is no higher authority. God's holiness means that He is separate from sin and incorruptible. Sin is anything that is a departure from God's moral standard. As a result, God hates sin and is repulsed by it. The Bible teaches that God is angry with the wicked every day (Psalm 7:11) and is so pure that evil cannot dwell with Him (Psalm 5:5; Habakkuk 1:13).

As an expression of His holiness, God delights in justice and will see to it that all wrongs are made right. He is a just judge, and His justice will be perfect, wise, and thorough. There is a coming Judgment Day when all the outstanding debts of men will be called to account (Acts 17:31).

But although He is holy and just, God is also "merciful and gracious, longsuffering, and abounding in goodness and truth" (Exodus 34:6). The Scriptures tell us He is compassionate, "slow to anger and abundant in lovingkindness" (Jonah 4:2). In fact, love is so much a part of His character that the Scriptures tell us, "God is love" (1 John 4:16).

This is the Almighty God to whom we will give an account on the Day of Judgment. It is for this reason that we find ourselves in our predicament, facing death. Let's allow the Bible, the key to our escape plan, to reveal to us our challenge and see if it indeed enables us to escape from death itself.

CHAPTER 3

ASSESSING OURSELVES

"We can easily forgive a child who is afraid of the dark; the real tragedy of life is when men are afraid of the light."
—PLATO

When I started as a young performer, I didn't have the financial backing that many others had. My father worked in a local factory and did woodworking to supplement his income. He was a good provider but was by no means a wealthy man. I had to learn how to be resourceful. Early in my career I decided that the addition of some fog to my performance would add a little theatrics and maybe even a bit of class and mystery. Not having the funds to purchase a real fog machine, I came up with a plan. If I was to buy the fog fluid and then purchase a bug fogger from the local hardware store, I would essentially have a fog machine! I reasoned that the bug fogger worked basically on the same principle and would save me quite a bit of money.

Luckily, I had the presence of mind to try the machine privately before ever attempting to use it publicly. In

ESCAPE OR DIE

the privacy of my own basement I began the experiment. Almost immediately, hot oily fluid came spewing from the end of the bug fogger and all over the walls. Not a drop became fog. My basement transformed into the scene of the worst oil spill since the Exxon Valdez.

You see, it's all about design. The bug fogger was never designed to be a fog machine. Understanding that fact would have saved me from a very unpleasant predicament! In the same way, death was not designed to be part of the natural order of things. It is an invader and unwelcome enemy (1 Corinthians 15:26). Understanding that fact will help us to be saved from a far worse predicament.

> Death was not designed to be part of the natural order of things. It is an invader and unwelcome enemy.

As we learned previously, evaluating our spiritual condition—just as with planning an escape—requires being honest with ourselves in assessing our strengths and weaknesses. Here are some of those "ugly truths" about ourselves that may be humbling, but are necessary to understand to save our lives.

Our Origin

God is the Creator of all things, and humans are His created beings, made in His image. The Bible says, "So God created man in His own image; in the image of God He created him; male and female He created them" (Genesis 1:27).

The Scriptures tell us that man was created from the dust of the ground. In the beginning Adam and Eve were in perfect fellowship with God. They enjoyed their Creator's presence as they walked in the garden. They were not only God's creation but were His friends.

Assessing Ourselves

Man was given free reign of the garden that was created for him. He was in charge of it and was given the responsibility of caring for it (Genesis 1:28). God gave man only one limitation to this vested authority: he was not to eat of a certain tree (Genesis 2:17), or he would die. That one tree was off-limits. In the same way that you want someone to love you because they want to and not because they have to, God gave man free moral agency or the ability to make choices. We are to love and obey our Creator, but for our love of God to be sincere, it cannot be forced. It needs to be a genuine expression of our heartfelt gratitude. In obeying God, we demonstrate our love for Him and acknowledge His gift of life and all He's given us to sustain it. As I often say, it's not obedience where there's no opportunity to be disobedient. At this time the earth was in perfect harmony. In the beginning even the animals were vegetarians; every beast of the earth was given plants for food (Genesis 1:30). There was no death or fear in the world. Mankind was in perfect fellowship with God and His creation.

Man-made Prison

Then the first man and woman made a choice. They chose to defy God and do the very thing they were warned not to do: they ate from that forbidden tree. The Scriptures clearly state, "The soul who sins shall die" (Ezekiel 18:4). Their act of rebellion, or sin, ushered death into the world that they were commissioned to care for.

When they sinned, they immediately died spiritually and that death sealed the fate of their physical bodies. Their bodies were sentenced to return to dust through death and labor was to be man's lot in life (Genesis 3:19). Humans had become bound in the shackles of sin and had created their own prison.

ESCAPE OR DIE

We would all like to believe otherwise but man's historical record bears it out: we are in a mess, and our world is in a mess. Creation itself is cursed by the effects of our misconduct and is described as being in "the bondage of corruption" (Romans 8:19–22). Earthquakes, floods, hurricanes, and tornadoes are just a few of the ways that nature has been twisted and altered by man's fall into sin. If it causes death and destruction, it's due to sin.

We can see evidence of this curse not only in our world, but in ourselves. Ever since mankind rebelled against God's authority, this trait of sin and defiance has been passed on to our offspring. That's why you never have to teach a child to lie; it just comes naturally. It's also why, when you tell little Johnny not to touch the hot stove, it doesn't take too long to hear a loud shout coming from the peanut gallery. Johnny burned his hand. Once we know something is forbidden, our rebellious nature wants to do it even more (Romans 7:11). The famous theologian Augustine when speaking about this inbred capacity for wrongdoing said, "The innocence of children is not so much due to the purity of their thoughts but the weakness of their limbs."

Conversely, because man was made in God's image, we are not devoid of all ethics and have established laws to govern ourselves to maintain peace and order. This innate desire for justice is also seen in small children. Try giving that same little Johnny only one piece of candy and his playmates two pieces. In mere seconds Johnny will rise up to point out the injustice. Our moral compass has been ravaged by sin yet retains enough function to recognize when we've been wronged. However, that same faculty lacks reliability in pointing out our own wrongdoing. It needs help. It needs to become aware.

Assessing Ourselves

Circle of Awareness

I was taught how to skydive by world champion skydiver and Olympic champion Roger Nelson in 1988. He was helping me to prepare for my aerial box escape—an unprecedented feat of escaping from a locked box thrown from an airplane. First, we began with training classes on the ground. I had to learn about the equipment, wind patterns, canopy flight, and emergency procedures. On the first few skydives, I was actually attached to the instructor in what is called a tandem jump. On this kind of jump, you are simply a passenger and the jump is designed to get you used to the environment. Initially, you experience what is referred to as "sensory overload"—the paralyzing experience of being almost frozen as your brain is trying to process all the unfamiliar information it's being bombarded with. Your instructor may even give you a "dummy" ripcord to see if you remember to pull it on your first jump. Often, students don't remember to pull, which is very sobering and helps them to take the subsequent lessons even more seriously.

When you finally get to the point of wearing your own parachute instead of sharing your instructor's giant one, you are on the way to becoming a real skydiver. These jumps involve the instructor holding on to you during the jump and using hand signals to communicate. This is where you are introduced to the "circle of awareness." The circle of awareness consists of the ground, your altimeter (a device on the wrist that measures altitude), and your instructor. This is a formal exercise that combats sensory overload and keeps the student mindful of the earth that is approaching at 180 miles per hour (mph). In time the student can associate by sight what the ground looks like at certain altitudes.

ESCAPE OR DIE

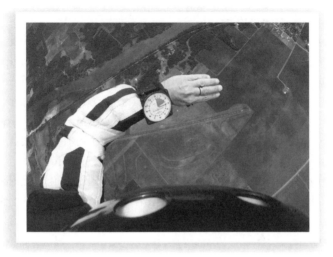

Checking the altimeter for altitude

In this freefall of life in which we all find ourselves, you want to ensure you land safely on the other side. To help you accomplish this, you are about to enter your spiritual "circle of awareness." In this circle of awareness, the ground represents the consequence of our freefall (death), the altimeter represents our conscience, and God's Word is our Instructor.

Your conscience can be of great benefit to you but, like an altimeter, won't do you a bit of good if you ignore it or if it's broken. Years ago, prior to one of my training jumps, I recall dropping my altimeter in the hangar before making my way out to the aircraft. Thinking nothing of the fumble, I put it on my wrist and boarded the airplane. Typically, as the airplane climbs to altitude, skydivers periodically check their altimeters to ensure that they are working. I noticed quickly that mine was no longer functioning. I could see out the window that the plane was climbing, but the needle of my altimeter remained motionless. We did the jump anyway and I shared my trainer's altimeter as he stuck his

Assessing Ourselves

wrist in my face every few thousand feet before parachute deployment.

If we listen to our conscience when confronted with the other elements of the circle of awareness (especially God's Word), it will give us a clear picture of the situation. If our conscience is broken, we will need help from our Instructor to gauge our true condition. Scripture talks about having a seared conscience, a weak conscience, and also a good conscience (1 Timothy 1:5). The fact that you can have a good conscience tells us that the conscience can also be damaged or warped as well. God's Word can revive it to function again on our behalf.

The following pages will require you to check with your altimeter (conscience). Please don't allow the sensory overload of the world or any preconceived notions to paralyze you. This is one exercise we all have to complete to survive.

The Shackles That Bind

We like to think of ourselves as being free to live however we please, but in reality that freedom is just an illusion. The Bible refers to those who commit sin as being "slaves" to sin (John 8:34). The word "slave" conveys some really disturbing imagery to our minds. It implies some form of control, handcuff, or shackle that prohibits freedom. That's bad enough, but often this lack of freedom is coupled with mistreatment and cruelty of the worst sort.

I have a collection of hundreds of handcuffs, jail locks, padlocks, safe locks, and restraints. Often it's difficult for people to understand why I would accumulate such a large array of items. A collection for an escape artist is an invaluable reference tool. When challenged to escape from a restraining device, ninety percent of the time I can go to my collection and produce the exact make and style of

ESCAPE or DIE

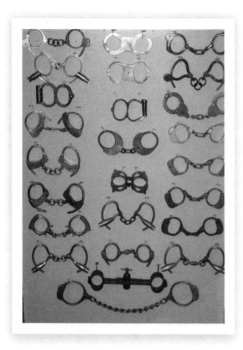

A handcuff board from the Anthony Collection

lock, handcuff, or restraint. If it's in my collection, I have already formulated a method to compromise the mechanism. If it's not in my collection, the experience I have gained from the other devices will carry me through the unfamiliar territory.

In this collection is a restraint called a spiked clog shackle. This device encircles one ankle and has large steel projections about 10 inches long on each side. This restraint has no adjustment. If you had a small ankle you were fortunate. If you had a large ankle the manacle was simply forced shut. As you might imagine, these conditions frequently resulted in vascular disease and amputations for those who were subjected to its brutality. The shackle was designed to impede a slave from running away as the spikes would grab and catch on everything they touch, causing the prisoner to stumble and fall.

We saw how the first man, Adam, rebelled against God and became bound by sin, and that all of humanity has followed in his steps. The Bible speaks of those who "shall stumble; they shall fall and be broken, be snared and taken" (Isaiah 8:15), and it warns us about "the sin which so easily ensnares us" (Hebrews 12:1). To understand what is

Assessing Ourselves

binding us personally—and how to be set free—we need to accurately assess our own situation. The first step in doing so is to look at our own "collection" and examine the shackles carefully. The following chapter has been prepared to help you do just that.

CHAPTER 4

THE MAN IN THE BOX

"Oh, where oh where can my baby be?
The Lord took her away from me
She's gone to heaven so I got to be good
So I can see my baby when I leave this world."
—WAYNE COCHRAN, "LAST KISS" LYRICS

People have a common misconception. As the above lyrics from a popular song of the 1960s would suggest, we've "got to be good" to get to Heaven. Most people think they've already met that criteria and will be the first in line at Heaven's gates. They obey the "Golden Rule," try to do what's right, and are productive members of society. They may be involved in philanthropic groups that feed and clothe the poor or educate underprivileged children. Yet their concept of what is "good" is often relative and dependent on individual opinion.

The Bible, however, tells us that "there is not a just man on the earth who does good and does not sin" (Ecclesiastes 7:20). There was a time I didn't think of myself as a sinner, at least not a very "bad" one. None of us like to think of ourselves in those terms. Most of us try to sanitize our

ESCAPE OR DIE

behavior by comparing ourselves to others or justifying why our sins aren't that bad.

In my travels I've had the privilege of befriending many law enforcement officers and criminologists. They tell me that even those we consider the worst among us don't see themselves as being bad. Richard "The Iceman" Kuklinski, the mob hit man who was personally responsible for the deaths of over a hundred people, wrote in a letter to a friend, "They call me a mass murderer —not that there is anything wrong with it. That doesn't make me a bad person." That man was once a playful little child, a mother's son, a brother, a boy of promise with his whole life ahead of him. The years of disobedience hardened his heart and finally robbed him of his freedom and any practical sense of right and wrong. Sin numbs and destroys our conscience.

> *Had I not known that I was just thrown from a plane in a locked box, I would have thought everything was fine.*

When I was locked in a box and thrown from an airplane, I can tell you as the man in the box there was no way to know I was plummeting toward the earth. It didn't even feel like I was falling. In the dark confines of the box I couldn't see and had I not known that I was just thrown from a plane in a locked box, I would have thought everything was fine.

You and I are not fine. We are in a deadly freefall, and we need God's Word to put windows in our box and show us we're in real trouble. It reminds us of our own mortality (we can see the clouds flying by now) and allows light to shine on our shackled hands. In doing so it removes all doubt that we're in bondage and proves to us the urgent need to be set free. Unlike most skydives, however, our altitude is never known in this particular race against death. Over 6,000 people die every hour and chances are most of them did not think it was their last hour.

Shining Light on Your Shackles

Jesus was once approached by a young man who desperately wanted to know what he must do to enter Heaven. The man asked, "Good Teacher, what shall I do that I may inherit eternal life?" Jesus first corrected the man's concept of good by saying, "Why do you call Me good? No one is good but One, that is, God" (Mark 10:17,18). Jesus then pointed him to God's standard of goodness, the Ten Commandments.

In the book of Exodus, God revealed these commandments, also known as the moral Law, to the Israelites as His standard for right living. Most of us are familiar with the Ten Commandments—or have at least heard of them—but we rarely allow them to search our hearts enough to see ourselves the way God sees us.

The first section of God's moral Law represents our relationship with God, while the second section shows us how we are to relate to each other. In Matthew 22:37–40 Jesus summarized the essence of the Law in two great commandments that God expects from mankind. He said, "'You shall love the Lord your God with all your heart, with all your soul, and with all your mind.' This is the first and great commandment. And the second is like it: 'You shall love your neighbor as yourself.' On these two commandments hang all the Law and the Prophets."

Evangelists of old made it a practice to use God's Law when presenting biblical truth because breaking the Law is sin (1 John 3:4), which is the root cause of death—both spiritual and physical. By letting God's standard search and judge us, it will show us the danger we're in and therefore is of great value. The apostle Paul went as far as to say that he wouldn't know what sin was if it wasn't for God's Law (Romans 7:7).

We are about to look closer at that standard and make it personal. Allowing the light of God's Law to shine in your box will help you to see the chains you're wearing. My hope and prayer is that you will tough this out and examine your own heart. You need to understand the shackles that bind you before you can escape.

The First Commandment addresses the position we give God in our lives.

1. "You shall have no other gods before Me." (Exodus 20:3)

As our Creator, God should be our first love and our highest priority. He has not only given us the gift of life and enabled us to appreciate His creation, but has provided us with all the things we enjoy, including our family, hobbies, talents, and so on. It's selfish for us to love the gifts more than the Giver.

Some people have made money, their careers, or myriad other transient objects their god. Whatever captures our greatest affections is our god, whether it be a silver golf club or a golden idol. God alone is worthy of our deepest affections.

The Scriptures tell us that no one has kept this commandment perfectly (Psalm 14:2,3). This is one shackle that is guaranteed to be locked firmly around the hands of each of us.

The Second Commandment may seem a bit foreign to us.

2. "You shall not make for yourself any carved image…; you shall not bow down to them nor serve them." (Exodus 20:4,5)

After all, how many of us have ever made an idol to worship? However, we can make idols not only with our hands but with our imaginations as well. People often imagine God as a grandfatherly figure who will gladly turn a blind eye to sin, or who is so loving He would never send anyone to Hell. This is not the case. Although He is love incarnate, God is also righteous and holy, and hates sin. His justice and holiness will not allow wrongdoing to go unpunished. Earlier we saw how some people are ensnared in belief systems that inaccurately portray the nature of God. We have to accept God as He has revealed Himself to us in the Bible. To picture Him in any other way is not only sin but is dangerous. It can cause us to make assumptions about God's nature that can lead to our ruin.

I'm told that on the stone temples of Madurai in southern India, there are more than a million carved images of gods and goddesses. Man has always had a fertile imagination. Unfortunately, the gods of our imagination can't hear us, help us, or save us. Only the one true God can save us from our sin. Have you created a god in your imagination that you're more comfortable with? That's called idolatry.

The Law, in its Third Commandment, then addresses the question: How often have you misused the name of God?

3. "You shall not take the name of the Lord your God in vain." (Exodus 20:7)

Our names represent who we are. In some cultures a name is more than a mere label. It speaks to the character and attributes of its bearer. When the Jewish patriarch Abraham introduced himself to people, he was in essence conveying, "I'm the father of many nations." That's because the name Abraham literally means "father of many nations" or "father of a multitude." That name was part and parcel of who he was. Similarly, God's name carries with it the majesty and authority of who He is. Using His name carelessly is a true sign of contempt, if not full-blown hatred. When we lose respect for the name, we disrespect the bearer as well.

The Jews so revered the name of God that they would not even say it out loud, let alone use it as a curse word as so many do today. It's called blasphemy when you use the name of God or Jesus Christ as a curse word to express anger or disgust, or exclaim "Oh my God" (or the ever-present "OMG") in surprise. Many don't think they're blaspheming because "it's just an expression," but that is the very point—they don't give the name of Almighty God any significance.

Have you ever misused God's name? The Bible clearly warns us, "The Lord will not hold him guiltless who takes His name in vain" (Exodus 20:7).

The Fourth Commandment is an effort to curb man's propensity to be caught up in the physical to the point of neglecting the spiritual.

4. "Remember the Sabbath day, to keep it holy." (Exodus 20:8)

Scripture tells us that, "Six days you shall do your work, but on the seventh day you shall rest" (Exodus 23:12). Remembering the Sabbath day helps to give us an opportunity to rest our bodies and thank God for His wondrous creation. In doing so, we acknowledge that God alone is the source of our sustenance. Even our hearts would cease to beat if it was not for God's care. Evangelist Billy Graham when commenting on this commandment mentions that God in His wisdom is telling us our bodies need this day for rest as our souls need it for worship.

God has seen fit to bless, supply, and protect us, despite the fact that man tends to ignore Him. Do you acknowledge God's provision by stopping to honor and thank Him?

I think the Fifth Commandment means more to me now, as an adult, than it did when I was young.

5. "Honor your father and your mother." (Exodus 20:12)
I have a greater respect for my parents now that I'm a little older and hopefully wiser. They sent me to a Christian school when it would have been more economical and convenient to do otherwise. They gave me food, clothing, and a roof over my head. They also tolerated my insane desire to be hung upside down in straitjackets and locked in steel safes. In retrospect, I should have been even more obedient and grateful for their instruction and patience when I was a youth.

The Fifth Commandment carries with it the idea of recognizing authority and having the willingness to submit to it. And this commandment is unique in that it also comes with a promise: "that your days may be long upon the land which the Lord your God is giving you" (Exodus 20:12). A sure sign of trouble ahead, however, is the individual who refuses to submit to authority and give due respect to rank or position (Exodus 22:28). Things will typically go well for us when we submit to the rules and laws of society. This principle is generally first learned and put into practice in the home—with our parents.

In honoring our parents we honor the One who provided them to us. Have you always honored your parents? If not, you need to ratchet another cuff to your ankle.

ESCAPE OR DIE

The Sixth Commandment prohibits the unlawful taking of human life.

6. "You shall not murder." (Exodus 20:13)

When we look at the prohibition against committing murder, most of us probably think that's one shackle too big to be placed on our wrists. But the Bible brings the commandment home when it likens hatred to murder: "Whoever hates his brother is a murderer, and you know that no murderer has eternal life abiding in him" (1 John 3:15). You see, God looks not just at our actions but at the thoughts and intents of the heart (Hebrews 4:12).

We are all transparent to God. With people we can often hide behind our masks and pretend to be something we're not. But if you have ever hated anyone or wished someone harm, God is aware of it. He even knows that the only boundaries preventing some people from acting on that hatred are the temporal punishments enforced by earthly governments. In the kingdom of God our hearts will stand trial in the most supreme of courts.

Have you ever broken the Sixth Commandment by harboring hatred toward someone? If so, God sees you as a murderer.

The Seventh Commandment is designed to preserve the sanctity of marriage.

7. "You shall not commit adultery." (Exodus 20:14)

Jesus confronted those who thought they were without sin when He said, "But I say to you that whoever looks at a woman to lust for her has already committed adultery with her in his heart" (Matthew 5:28). Like with the preceding commandment, we are again confronted with sins of the heart. Ever stop to think that every act you have ever committed started inside (as a thought) before it was birthed outside (as an action)? People who look at pornography may never physically act out what they've seen; nevertheless, their hearts are filled with grievous sin—whether it's acted on or not.

It's not uncommon for people to agree that adultery is wrong but miss the fact that *all* sexual activity outside of marriage—including fornication (sex between unmarried people)—is sin and is forbidden by God. The Bible says, "Flee sexual immorality. Every sin that a man does is outside the body, but he who commits sexual immorality sins against his own body" (1 Corinthians 6:18).

Sexual sin is a powerful and destructive enemy, partly because it takes what was meant by God to be a beautiful gift and warps its intent and expression. The natural desire to have sexual relations is God-given, yet its lawful outlet needs to be confined within the sanctity of marriage. The heartbreak and disease that are known to result from violating this command should help us to see why God warns us to flee from its snare. Many mighty men have been brought low by this formidable enemy. Have you ever looked with lust? Fornicators and adulterers will not inherit the kingdom of God.

Next, Commandment number eight speaks of the sin of stealing.

8. "You shall not steal." (Exodus 20:15)

Over my many years as an escape artist I've been known to do some jail time. Usually it's under ten minutes—but jail time nonetheless. I've escaped from jails that have connections with some of the most infamous crime figures in history, including John Dillinger and Baby Face Nelson. When we think of stealing we may think of such notorious men. But how much do you have to steal to earn the label of "thief"? I think you'd agree the dollar amount is irrelevant. If you've ever taken anything that doesn't belong to you, you're guilty of stealing. We can even steal ideas, software, and other intangibles.

Sometimes I think about how my life would be different if everyone were perfectly honest. As a Registered Safe Technician, I'm occasionally called on to open antique safes for which people have lost the combinations. Locks were developed to keep people honest. We wouldn't need safes, locks, or handcuffs if people didn't have the desire to steal.

I remember watching an old Gary Cooper movie years ago. (Older films seem to have a charm that their newer counterparts tend to lack. It seems more time was spent on quality stories instead of fiery explosions and other diversionary eye candy.) In the 1941 movie *Meet John Doe*, Gary Cooper says, "I'm gonna talk about us—the average guys, the John Does." He goes on to say, "He's got a streak of larceny in his heart." The writers were right about that—we do have a streak of larceny in our heart, yet the Scriptures pointed it out long before John Doe did.

Have you ever stolen anything, regardless of the value? If so, you are a thief, and the Bible says that thieves will not enter Heaven (1 Corinthians 6:10).

Commandment Nine teaches us that our "little white lies" aren't so little.

9. "You shall not bear false witness against your neighbor." (Exodus 20:16)

Lies are the truth seeker's enemy, and we should want no part in telling or even hearing them. In an effort to minimize the weight of our chains, we often justify our lies by calling them "little white lies" or describing them as "exaggerations." These attempts to dodge responsibility for lying reveal our inner willingness to deceive. Gossip, slander, and false testimony have destroyed many reputations and lives. Scripture tells us that "lying lips are an abomination to the Lord" (Proverbs 12:22) because lies are in direct opposition to God's nature. The Bible tells us that it is impossible for God to lie (Hebrews 6:18). Author and humorist Mark Twain is quoted as saying, "A man is never more truthful than when he acknowledges himself a liar."

Have you ever told a lie? The Bible is very clear about what happens to those who have broken this commandment: "All liars shall have their part in the lake which burns with fire..." (Revelation 21:8).

Last, the Tenth Commandment warns us not to covet.

10. "You shall not covet your neighbor's house; you shall not covet your neighbor's wife, nor his manservant, nor his maidservant, nor his ox, nor his donkey, nor anything that is your neighbor's." (Exodus 20:17)

Coveting is jealously desiring something that belongs to someone else. You can covet people's wealth, their position, their home, or even their spouse. At its very core, covetousness is a lack of contentment and gratitude with what God has already blessed you with. It in effect says to God, "You didn't give me enough. I deserve more." In reality, after going through the Commandments with me, you are probably beginning to see what we really deserve. It certainly isn't more blessings. What we rightly deserve is punishment!

So, how did you do? Like the rest of us, you have probably found that you've violated at least some of the Ten Commandments. Yet you may still think you'll be okay if you've broken only a few. To see the seriousness of your predicament, consider what the Bible says: "For whoever shall keep the whole law, and yet stumble in one point, he is guilty of all" (James 2:10). Think of yourself suspended over a chasm, hanging onto a chain of ten links, when one of the links breaks. You are just as doomed as if all of them have broken. But very likely you have violated God's Laws more than once. Stop to consider: How many times have you looked with lust? How many lies have you told in your life? How many times have you used God's name in vain, or enjoyed the gift of another day of life without giving your Creator the priority He deserves?

You have not just committed an occasional crime here and there, but if you are honest you will see that you are guilty of committing *thousands* of crimes against a holy God. You don't have merely a shackle or two loosely bound around your wrists that you can easily slip out of; you are in fact firmly shackled and bound by sin! Humans by our nature are indeed slaves to sin.

But, some may argue, what if your sins were committed long ago? God's standards have no expiration date. Laws and taboos among societies may shift and change, yet God's expectations do not. Unlike our courts of law, there is no statute of limitations with God, and time does not forgive sin. Don't be misled; nobody makes a fool out of God (Galatians 6:7). Sin is sure to be judged. We are promised that, because of these things, the wrath of God is coming (Ephesians 5:6). It is only God's mercy and patience that prevent immediate justice from falling on our heads.

Psychologists try to tell us that "I'm OK, you're OK," but the fact of the matter is we're not OK. We all like to think we're good, but when we look at God's holy standard, we see that we are not good at all—we are sinners. It takes courage to accurately assess ourselves and admit we're sinners. To admit I was a sinner was to acknowledge that I was in rebellion to God. Scripture actually states we are enemies of God because of our wicked works (Colossians 1:21). Even worse, if I am His enemy, it would follow then that I'm at war with Almighty God!

Such a thought horrified me! Then someone introduced me to these laws and they humbled me and convicted my conscience. Such knowledge broke my heart and made me desperate to end that war. I may not have been a mass murderer, but I had become aware that I was God's enemy nonetheless.

At funerals we often hear canned consolation phrases like "He's in a better place now," or "She is with the angels now." Scripture, however, says we need to be holy to enter Heaven (Hebrews 12:14). That means to be perfect in goodness or, said another way, to be morally and ethically pure. If you are not holy (sinless) before the Judge of the universe, you are not going to Heaven. If you are not holy, only judgment awaits you.

Awaiting Judgment

Martin Luther said, "Every man must do two things alone; he must do his own believing and his own dying." Some people are fatalistic about their own mortality—they believe they are not accountable to any God, and see death as the conclusion of their existence. In Edgar Allan Poe's poem "The Conqueror Worm," he concludes by saying, "The play is the tragedy 'Man' and its hero the Conqueror Worm." Others use humor in a vain attempt to whistle through the graveyard. The comedian Woody Allen is quoted as saying, "I don't want to achieve immortality through my work. I want to achieve immortality by not dying." We chuckle at that, but like all "gallows humor," the concept of death still makes us squirm.

ESCAPE or DIE

Instinctively, deep in the recesses of our hearts, we all know there will be a day of reckoning. Our innate sense of justice demands it.

Houdini's 1926 tour in which he exposed fraudulent spirit mediums carried the tagline "Do Spirits Return?" Scripture gives us clear answers to that question. Spirits of the dead cannot return to earth and any hint of reincarnation is a lie. Instead, we are told that man will die once and stand before God to be judged (Hebrews 9:27).

Most world religions teach that God weighs our good deeds against our bad and if we have done more good than bad, we are safe. The Bible does not teach this, and in fact, even intellectually that argument doesn't make sense. Let's imagine I was to be convicted in federal court for a heinous murder. At the sentencing I quickly point out to the judge how I faithfully rang the kettle bell for the Salvation Army for the past ten years and therefore deserve to be forgiven. Sounds ridiculous, doesn't it? That's because it *is* ridiculous, and our own inner sense of right and wrong concedes that crimes should be punished. It doesn't matter how many good deeds criminals may have done; they are still held accountable for the laws they've broken.

We, like Adam, have broken God's moral Laws and created our own prison. We are firmly shackled and in the freefall of sin. We are guilty and deserve punishment. What awaits us at the end of this—the ultimate freefall?

CHAPTER 5

TRUTH OR CONSEQUENCES

*"Everybody, soon or late, sits down to
a banquet of consequences."*
—ROBERT LOUIS STEVENSON

When a skydiver is under an open parachute, he is restricted to what instructors call "the cone of maneuverability." This is where the prevailing winds and the forward speed of the parachute determine how far one can stray from the drop zone and still end up in the landing area. This is important, as straying from the drop zone can lead to many dangers just as bad as hitting the ground at 180 mph. Power lines, ponds, highways, trees, and fences are just a few of the potential hazards that can turn a parachute ride into an ambulance ride.

Just as there are natural laws—such as gravity—that when violated have consequences, so do the moral Laws that we just examined. It matters little if we disagree with these laws or even believe they exist; like simple laws of physics, they are real and are violated at our peril.

Most of my escapes carry some consequence for failure. Some are extreme, such as hitting the ground at 180

ESCAPE OR DIE

mph or suffocating in some predicament like the sand-filled cangue. Others are not as severe and would only leave me defeated and professionally embarrassed, like a failed jail escape. As we consider how this relates spiritually, we're confronted with the realization that the stakes are too high and the price too dreadful to fail this escape. There are things far worse than physical death. Failure cannot be an option here.

As I share the following experiences, please think about how this relates to your spiritual condition. I can't think of a more serious consequence than where we will spend eternity.

The Canyon

Generally speaking, I don't like to travel. Some people just want to get away to go somewhere new or see some sights. My travel escapes tend to take a different form. My trip to Idaho was no exception. I was going there for something unprecedented: I was on my way to leap from an aircraft, bound and shackled, over the Snake River Canyon. The goal was to escape from the handcuffs in freefall with enough time to deploy my parachute and then safely land on the canyon's north rim. The trip there, though, felt almost as dangerous as the stunt. The next time you fly coach and the ride gets a little bumpy, you can comfort yourself with this story.

We needed to use a particular type of aircraft for the canyon stunt so we decided it was easier to bring our own than to try to find one in Idaho. We would then not only have our own jump plane but we could save money on airfares from Chicago to Idaho. The Twin Otter aircraft we used is popular among skydivers for its versatility and reliability. Nevertheless, the Otter does have some weaknesses to consider when using it for travel. Because the plane

Truth or Consequences

is not a jet (it has propellers), comparatively speaking, it travels very slowly. Skydiving airplanes have also had the seats removed and rubber mats put in their place. Having to sit on the floor is fine when you're wearing a parachute and using the plane as an elevator, but stinks when you're using the plane for transportation—especially for such a long flight. It makes for an especially uncomfortable ride. As if that's not bad enough, these airplanes do not have pressurized cabins. That means supplemental oxygen must be used at altitude to prevent hypoxia. Hypoxia is a condition that starves the brain of oxygen and can cause confusion, disorientation, and bad judgment (most people think I am a chronic sufferer). So we flew for eight hours from Chicago to Idaho with no seats, no peanuts, and no movies, and wearing gas masks to breathe the supplemental oxygen. As we passed over the Colorado Rocky Mountains, snow flew in the cracks of the cabin door and I prayed that if there would be any

Shackled and ready for the canyon

problems with the aircraft they wouldn't happen there. To go down in the mountains, even armed with parachutes, was an experience I would rather leave to my imagination. Thankfully, we arrived without incident.

ESCAPE OR DIE

The Jerome County Commissioners Office purchased the handcuffs I was to use, and a certified bonded locksmith examined them and verified they were legitimate and unaltered. The handcuffs were then sealed in an evidence bag and locked in the county commissioner's vault. We had to schedule the jump for 7:00 a.m. because the wind would be the calmest at that time of day. I am not a morning person, so to say I was not pleased with the time would be an understatement.

The Sheriff's Office had given us a boat ride the day before to view the site and explained that portions of the river that run through the canyon are wild and untamed, and certain areas of the canyon are virtually inaccessible. If I or the cameramen who'd accompany me were to drift there by parachute, it would mean our doom. There would be nothing they could do to save us. There are also deadly vortexes scattered randomly throughout the river. These vortexes, like a reverse tornado, would suck us violently underwater in an instant. Falling into one of these would be the absolute end with no hope of escape. Even a fully equipped scuba diver will perish if he's swallowed by a vortex.

> *Falling into one of these deadly vortexes would be the absolute end with no hope of escape.*

Our landing promised to be nerve-racking enough even if we successfully avoided the chasm below. The Idaho terrain surrounding the canyon looked like a lunar landscape. Unlike the wide open field at the drop zone in Chicago, we would have to steer clear of the large boulders and rocks that would most certainly greet us upon landing. It's said that sticks and stones will break your bones, and I

Truth or Consequences

had no intention of proving that little childhood ditty to be true.

The morning of the jump came quickly. We met representatives from the Sheriff's Office, Jerome County Search and Rescue, as well as a group of reporters and cameramen at the local airport. I slipped my jumpsuit on while my partner, Roger Nelson, demonstrated that my parachute's automatic opening device was disabled. In other words, technology would not resolve a failed escape attempt. I had to escape in roughly 30 seconds to deploy my chute, or face the consequences at the bottom of the canyon. I would either be "World Champion Escape Artist" or remnants on a rock. We slipped our parachutes on and the pilot started the Twin Otter. The evidence bags containing the restraints were opened and their contents were locked about my wrists and arms. We boarded the airplane, accepted the well wishes of our hosts, and took to the clear Idaho sky.

Just before we reached altitude and were ready to jump, we realized that Roger's goggles had somehow been misplaced. He assured me this was not a problem; still, I was not convinced and worried that Roger would be unable to see at terminal velocity. But there was no time to regroup—it was now or never. We had practiced and coordinated the timing of our jump so that Roger could grab my ankles upon exiting the aircraft and fall with me. Roger's helmet-mounted camera could then supply viewers with camera angles that would be difficult to capture by other methods. Roger's son, Matthew, an expert skydiver in his own right, was to jump with us and act as an additional freefall cameraman. The Otter door was opened and we began our cadence and count. *Ready, set, go...*

Our ankle grab went as planned and I was relieved when we settled into a stable freefall formation. So far,

ESCAPE OR DIE

Roger's eyes had not been blown out of their sockets and I was able to spring open the first handcuff shortly after we reached terminal velocity. I freed both hands quickly and began working on the chain that encircled my neck and upper arms. However, my fingers had grown numb in the chilly, high-velocity air and had lost their deftness, so I decided to deploy my parachute and finish the job on the way down when I had more time. All of our parachutes opened properly and we effectively steered clear of the gaping sepulcher that is the Snake River Canyon. As I gently floated to earth and enjoyed the silence, I noticed beyond us a well-manicured golf course. I smiled as it reminded me of my grandpa who enjoyed golf and had purchased for me those very first locks I had learned from so many years ago.

I chose the Snake River Canyon because, as a youngster in the 1970s, I saw Evel Knievel try to jump it in his "Skycycle" and dreamed of doing something similar. My jump was successful, in that I escaped my shackles in time to open my parachute and not plummet to the bottom of the canyon. Evel Knievel, on the other hand, had a malfunction and failed to breach the gap. Luckily for him, he missed the river vortex and landed on some nearby rocks. I jumped above it; he tried to jump across. In looking at the distance across the canyon I was reminded how far our sin has separated us from God. When I looked at the bottom of the chasm I was reminded of the penalty for dying in our sins.

The Chasm Below

If we've been honest in our examination of God's Law, we will admit that we are all bound by the shackles of sin and are guilty before God (Romans 3:19). We are in a deadly freefall, unable to free ourselves, and face a horrifying fate below. Yet for some inexplicable reason, some people insist they are not falling. Others may admit that they are falling, but their pride leads them to quickly point out how others have jumped from much higher altitudes; therefore, their jump isn't as bad as everyone else's. They forget that the length of the fall is not the final judgment—it's the sudden stop at the end we should be concerned with. That stop will not only be death—but our souls will be sent to a terrible place the Bible calls Hell.

Hell is a real, literal place, and like the river vortexes at the bottom of that canyon, it will be the absolute end with no hope of escape. It is described as a place of torment and everlasting punishment. The Bible teaches, "It is a fearful thing to fall into the hands of the living God" (Hebrews 10:31). Hell is the eternal prison for those who persist in their rebellion and reject the pardon offered by God. It is a place reserved not only for murderers and rapists but for fornicators, thieves, and all liars as well.

The Scriptures warn us that in Hell there will be weeping and gnashing of teeth and unquenchable fire (Matthew 13:50; Mark 9:43). It further warns that "the smoke of their torment ascends forever and ever; and they have no rest day or night" (Revelation 14:11). The ultimate despair and loss is found in this prison called Hell. It is a jail without parole or reprieve from regret, where the crushing burden of sin is felt forever.

I'm not telling you this just to scare you—although it certainly should. Jesus explained that Hell is so horrifying that if your eye or hand causes you to sin, it would be better to pluck out your eye or cut off your hand than to go there (Matthew 18:8,9). Just like the Jerome County sheriff warned me about the vortexes, I need to warn you about Hell. The sheriff would have been doing me a great disservice by not warning me of the real dangers I would be facing. He

ESCAPE or DIE

could be removed from office and charged with not fulfilling his oath to serve and protect citizens. In the same way, you need to be made aware that Hell exists and why people go there. You need to know the penalty for failing to escape —and I need to faithfully warn you.

Billy Graham said we really don't break God's commandments, as much as we break ourselves on them. A gentleman from my local gym recently told me a story that I'd like to share with you. He was returning to his vehicle on a particularly frosty afternoon one Wisconsin winter. In the course of doing so, he lost his footing and fell hard on the ice. He was carrying a briefcase at the time and managed to land squarely on top of it. Getting to his feet, he hobbled the rest of the way to his car. The searing pain in his side convinced him that he had broken a rib or two so he drove himself to the hospital for a checkup. The attending physician took X-rays and examined him thoroughly. The doctor calmly sat him down and was able to assure him that no ribs had been broken; nonetheless there was bad news to be had. A spot was found on his lung. That spot was later to be diagnosed as first-stage lung cancer. The doctor informed the man how genuinely fortunate he was to have caught it so early and that operations at this stage are highly successful.

As I listened to him tell his story, I detected a real sense of gratitude in his voice. He had dodged a bullet and he knew it. I was speaking to the only man I ever met who was grateful for falling on the ice.

Examining sin and its consequences can sometimes feel like falling on that hard ice. The truth can hurt, yet if you're still breathing, we caught it early enough. Now that you have the accurate diagnosis, you just need the cure.

CHAPTER 6

ONE WAY OUT

*"How shall we escape
if we neglect so great a salvation?"*
—HEBREWS 2:3

As an escape artist I have found it to be in my best interest to have several methods of escape at my disposal. Sometimes a restraint will prohibit me from employing my favorite method but will succumb to a different tactic that I've developed. One such episode occurred in Illinois when I was challenged to escape from a pair of handcuffs that had the keyholes brazed shut. Under normal circumstances I would simply reject such handcuffs as being altered or sabotaged. My general rule is to use only factory-produced restraints that meet universal police standards. But when I examined these cuffs I noticed something. Unbeknown to the welder, the brazing process had weakened the shackle springs. I merely rapped the cuffs on a hard surface and the double locks unlocked. This discovery enabled me to still do the escape and leave the police and reporters who were present at the event completely baffled. Such presentations to the uninitiated appear to be almost magic. We, of course, know different.

ESCAPE OR DIE

The fact of the matter is, sometimes there is only one way out. In those cases I accept the limitation and operate under the constraints the situation demands. A prime example is the aerial box escape that I briefly mentioned in Chapter 3. There was no backup plan, and no second chance, if I was unable to escape in time. Let's take a look at that aerial box escape in more detail.

The Great Escape

The year was 1988; at twenty-two years of age I was a brash, confident, albeit young escape artist on a life-or-death mission. I was about to show the world who was the "Greatest Escape Artist of All Time" in one huge, Herculean effort. Handcuffed and locked in a coffin-like box, I was to be thrown from an airplane at 13,500 feet, a height close to ten times that of the Empire State Building. The proposed task would be to complete an escape from the box in freefall, to skydive away from the plummeting missile, and to deploy my parachute before impact. This escape attempt would be only my seventeenth parachute jump, a fact that made most seasoned skydivers cringe. I had announced to the Associated Press my intent to do this escape before making even a single parachute jump, and now with fewer than a dozen and a half jumps I was ready to cheat death.

During my skydiving training I had overheard some of the expert jumpers doubting the improbable feat. They knew that, unlike a magician, I did not use handcuffs and locks that were altered to facilitate escape. This knowledge, coupled with the absence of "emergency plans," created a somber atmosphere at the drop zone. Even members of my own team encouraged me to bow out gracefully, citing two skydiving fatalities that had occurred only a few weeks before.

My initial observation of the sport was equally dis-

One Way Out

heartening as I watched a jumper put his foot through the windshield of a parked car just a few yards in front of me. Stubborn and determined, I knew overconfidence could kill but felt I was operating within my ability.

Though new to skydiving I had been listed in Ripley's Believe It or Not! as the "King of Escapists," a title I had earned through my jail cell escapes. Experienced in both underwater and land escapes, I went into the attempt knowing my first aerial escape could be my last.

Finally, the moment of truth arrived. Certified locksmiths verified the handcuffs and locks before they would be put

Anthony prior to the aerial box escape

to use. I strapped on a parachute and helmet, took a few deep breaths, and stretched out my hands. Several pairs of handcuffs were clamped on my wrists and I lay down inside the coffin-like box. The lid was closed and locked shut (with a double-sided Mosler lock) while I, inside, gritted my teeth refusing to back down. The Skyvan aircraft roared into the sky as my family agonized on the ground. My trainer, Roger Nelson, and another skydiver were to jump with the box and prevent it from spinning in the air. The centrifugal force of a spin could keep me a prisoner even if I were to defeat all the locks successfully. The jumpers

ESCAPE OR DIE

reaffirmed to each other that if I wasn't out by 2,000 feet, they would release the box and save themselves. I heard their affirmation.

The air was getting thinner as we approached altitude, so I did my best to breathe gently and conserve oxygen. Then the announcement was made that we had reached jump altitude and would begin the escape attempt. The jumpers began their countdown sequence: *Five, four, three, two, one.* The box was launched into space, and I was thrust into the biggest test of my career. Seconds hung like hours as I paused for the box to settle into freefall and terminal velocity. I began to work feverishly inside the box, systematically defeating each lock just as I had done hundreds of times on the ground. Keeping my complete attention focused on the task, the cuffs were off with 25 seconds left.

One way out: The box containing Anthony in freefall

The door lock succumbed to my workmanlike attack, and I heaved my body against its hardwood bracing. I swooped from my falling prison and welcomed the cool August air that greeted me. Relying on Roger's expert teaching, I skydived away from the box and deployed my parachute. Gently floating to earth, I screamed my victory and accepted the plaudits of those watching.

While I successfully cheated death on this attempt, the aerial box escape required two primary steps to succeed: I had to escape from the handcuffs and box, and then deploy my parachute before it was too late. In our spiritual freefall, we have the same tasks we must accomplish to make our great escape.

Although we're bound by sin and justly deserve the consequence of death and Hell, God's mercy, love, and grace are as great as His justice. That is why He provided a means for our escape. But like my aerial box escape, there is no backup plan, and no second chance—there is only one way out: the way He provided.

Good Deeds and Arm Flapping

Most people have the tendency to want to fix things themselves in their own power. Our culture has songs that celebrate the fact that "We did it our way." Our fast food restaurants guarantee that "you can have it your way." The Bible, however, tells us that our way, though self-gratifying, leads to death (Proverbs 16:25). Often people think they can do enough religious works or good deeds that will erase their sins and gain them entry to Heaven. Nothing could be further from the truth. That would be as crazy as jumping from an airplane without a parachute—but with a really good arm-flapping plan. Now, some people will be able, by self-will and determination, to flap their arms more rapidly than others. In the final analysis, though, no one will be able to tell by the greasy spot on the ground who the world champion arm-flapper was.

ESCAPE OR DIE

Essentially, all the world's man-made religions incorporate some form of arm flapping. They attempt to earn or merit favor with God by doing good things or trying to "bribe" God for their wrongdoing. I want to be very clear on this. It is impossible for you to clean up your own life in order to make yourself acceptable to God. It's not your actions that are the problem—it's your heart. Your actions are merely the symptom, not the cause. The Bible tells us that "from within, out of the heart of men, proceed evil thoughts, adulteries, fornications, murders, thefts, covetousness, wickedness, deceit, lewdness, an evil eye, blasphemy, pride, foolishness" (Mark 7:21,22). Even if it were possible for us to force ourselves into a strict regimen of right living, our hearts would still remain corrupt and unacceptable to God. Some people think that, despite their sins, they'll be okay with God "because He knows my heart." It's true, He does know our hearts. And He says the heart is "deceitful above all things, and desperately wicked" (Jeremiah 17:9).

Only God can remedy the root cause of a sinful heart and enable us to live right. This is why Scripture says, "I will give you a new heart and put a new spirit within you; I will take the heart of stone out of your flesh and give you a heart of flesh" (Ezekiel 36:26).

If you keep trying to flap your arms you'll eventually run out of altitude and you will perish. Ultimately, it's not God's will that should happen to you. Arm flapping is the last throes of pride in the guilty individual. We have been humbled enough to know we have sinned but not enough to realize that we are sinful creatures by our very nature and unable to fix things ourselves. Spiritually, there is only one way to escape the penalty for our sins. I pray that you will take it.

One Way Out

Let's look at how this escape plan plays out in the spiritual realm. The first step is to get out of what is binding us.

The 180-Degree Turn

While training for a handcuffed jump in Lake Wales, Florida, I heard a voice yelling at me as I was descending under my open parachute: "Right turn! Right turn!" My trainer was desperately trying to get my attention over the chest-mounted radio I was wearing. The winds had changed and I was approaching some dangerous obstacles. I listened to his advice and steered the parachute as instructed. Similarly, the Scriptures are desperately trying to get our attention, imploring us to make the right turn of repentance (Acts 17:30). Repentance is described as a 180-degree turn from our sins.

God's plan for man has never changed: He wants us to live forever in perfect relationship with Him, but our sin is preventing us from having fellowship with a holy God. Jesus said, "Unless you repent you will all likewise perish" (Luke 13:3). Yet Scripture assures us that God is patient and doesn't want anyone to perish; instead, He desires that all would turn to Him in an attitude of repentance (2 Peter 3:9). Repentance is

Steering the parachute for a safe landing

best understood as a change of mind that results in a change of behavior.

The following actions and attitudes accompany biblical repentance:

Acknowledge the sin: You must see yourself as a lost, desperately wicked sinner without hope, headed for death and God's prison: Hell. If you're not convinced yet, please go back to Chapter 4 and read it again. In repentance, you will not only see yourself as a sinner and will admit it, but you will recognize the fact that you have sinned against a holy God. Our sins are primarily "vertical"; even when we sin against other people, we are really sinning against God, because in rebelling against the rules He established we are rejecting His authority. Our circle of awareness helps us to see our true state. If your conscience is working, it will convict you of your sins; you simply need to be honest and confess your guilt. The Bible promises, "He who covers his sins will not prosper, but whoever confesses and forsakes them will have mercy" (Proverbs 28:13).

Hate the sin: The book of Jeremiah says of those who rebelled against God, "Were they ashamed when they had committed abomination? No! They were not at all ashamed; nor did they know how to blush" (Jeremiah 6:15). Today many openly defy the Laws of God without even the slightest sense of shame. When you see yourself as God sees you, however, you are brought to a place where there is godly sorrow for your sin. This is different from being sorry you were caught. When you think of all the things you have done over your lifetime in rebellion to your Creator, "you shall loathe [yourself] in your own sight because of all the evils that you have committed" (Ezekiel 20:43). In true repentance, there is the desire not only to escape the consequences of sin, but to be rid of the things that displease God.

One Way Out

Flee from sin: Repentance involves turning away from our sin. The Bible says, "Let the wicked forsake his way, and the unrighteous man his thoughts; let him return to the Lord, and He will have mercy on him; and to our God, for He will abundantly pardon" (Isaiah 55:7).

It is God's will that you forsake what you want Him to forgive. Consider this illustration. A well-known state governor was visiting a prison while in disguise. He fell into a discussion with an engaging young prisoner and considered giving him a full pardon. "What would you do if you were fortunate enough to obtain a pardon?" he asked. The prisoner, not recognizing the famous politician, replied, "If I ever get out of here, I'll cut the throat of the judge who sent me here." The governor left the cell stunned. To pardon a killer who had not changed his ways would be to let a monster loose on society.

Remember our tiny troublemaker, little Johnny (from Chapter 3)? Now the young rebel will not sit down in the classroom and is creating quite a disturbance. His teacher has told him repeatedly that he must be seated like everyone else. Johnny simply will not do it. The teacher tells Johnny she will have to report him to the principal and send him home if he persists in being so stubborn. Little Johnny, persuaded by the threat, finally sits down with an ear-to-ear grin on his face. This annoys the teacher even more and she asks him what he finds to be so amusing. Johnny says, "I may be sitting down on the outside, but I'm standing up on the inside." True repentance wants to sit down on the inside—from the heart.

Sometimes, though, all we can do is come to God with the "desire to be rid of the desire" for sin. It is scriptural to ask the Lord to incline our hearts to Him (Psalm 141:4) or said another way, to give us the "want to." The Bible

ESCAPE OR DIE

says God resists the proud but gives grace to the humble (James 4:6), and He is quick to forgive us when we are transparent, honest, and humble before Him. The desire to turn away from all known sin is true repentance. Repentance toward God unfastens our shackles and is the first step to defeating death.

We're not home free yet, however. We are still headed for that chasm unless we complete the second step in our escape plan. So far we've discussed everything but the most obvious and necessary element, without which survival would be impossible. Only one thing can save us from the freefall we are in: we need a parachute.

> *We're not home free yet, however. Only one thing can save us from the freefall we are in: we need a parachute.*

For our escape from death, God has provided a perfect Parachute for us in Jesus Christ. We will find out who He is and what He did for us in the next chapter.

CHAPTER 7

THE PERFECT PARACHUTE

*"Amazing grace! how sweet the sound
That saved a wretch like me!
I once was lost, but now am found,
Was blind, but now I see."*

—JOHN NEWTON, "AMAZING GRACE"

In order to satisfy His own sinless standard, God provided us a way to escape the penalty of our sin. The means of rescue God provided is called the gospel, or good news. And it is very good news! You may have heard it before in John 3:16, one of the most familiar verses of Scripture: "For God so loved the world that He gave His only begotten Son, that whoever believes in Him should not perish but have everlasting life." Jesus, the Son of God, is the only way to escape death once and for all.

The Pin Check

Before skydivers board an aircraft and right before they jump, they perform what is called a pin check. This check is done to verify that the parachute's harness straps are routed correctly and that the pins securing the parachute are

ESCAPE OR DIE

in place. The pilot chute that actually deploys the main canopy is also checked to make sure it is properly stowed and jump ready.

Before entrusting our life to a parachute, we need to examine it to ensure it is trustworthy. Parachutes have undergone hundreds of years of development. The terrible price of this learning curve is that mistakes are usually discovered only after a tragedy has occurred. We can't afford to experiment with our immortal souls. In the case of our spiritual escape, our decision will have eternal consequences. So let's check to see why Jesus is the perfect Parachute that God has provided.

This is where the rubber meets the road and we separate Christianity from other religions. Some religions claim Jesus was the spirit brother of Satan; others say He was an archangel, a created being, one of countless incarnations of a "Christ power," or just a good teacher. Knowing His true identity is so important that Jesus warned us about the many "false christs" who would come (Matthew 24:24). The apostle Paul also warned that people would attempt to preach another Jesus (2 Corinthians 11:4). It's like the difference between a back pack and a parachute. You can call the back pack a parachute all you want; however, the jump will reveal the truth. You need to have the correct Jesus. Trusting in a man-made Jesus cannot save you. It is nothing short of spiritual suicide. So what makes Jesus unique?

As we saw earlier, when Adam chose to rebel against God, he brought sin into the world. We therefore needed a second Man to correct the path the first man had set us on. The Scriptures tell us that the penalty for Adam's sin—and ours—is death, and that sin cannot be forgiven without the shedding of blood (Hebrews 9:22). Justice demands that the penalty be paid. God couldn't just turn a blind

The Perfect Parachute

eye to our crimes or He would be unjust and corrupt. So to make a way for sinful humanity to be forgiven, God decided to pay our sin debt Himself.

That's why God became a man in Jesus Christ. Jesus was literally God in the flesh—not "a god" but God Himself in human form (John 1:14). In Jesus Christ, Scripture says, the whole fullness of God dwelt in physical form (Colossians 1:19). He was conceived in a virgin's womb with no biological earthly father. God's Word says when speaking of the birth of Jesus Christ: "For unto us a Child is born, unto us a Son is given; and the government will be upon His shoulder. And His name will be called Wonderful, Counselor, Mighty God, Everlasting Father, Prince of Peace" (Isaiah 9:6). Jesus, who was never shackled by sin, lived the perfect, sinless life that we should have lived. He performed countless miracles, healed the sick, and even raised the dead, showing that He was God and had power over His creation. He was then put to death by being nailed to a Roman cross, incurring the death penalty in our place. God loves us so much that, even while we were His enemies, Jesus Christ willingly became our substitute (Romans 5:8,10). Jesus was bound for our sin (John 18:12), beaten for our sin (John 19:1), and crucified for our sin (John 19:18).

Not only did Jesus Christ die for you, during those moments He was on the cross He was forsaken by God the Father so you wouldn't have to be (Matthew 27:46). This is where the true pain of the cross took place. Just before He died on the cross, Jesus declared, "It is finished!" (John 19:30). He said this to announce that the sin debt had been settled. With His life's blood, He paid the ransom required to buy us out from under sin's bondage, once and for all (Hebrews 9:12). In this way God satisfied His own justice, and since the penalty for sin has now been paid, He offers the guilty the opportunity to be set free. This is why the gospel is such good news: "For the wages of sin is death, but the gift of God is eternal life in Christ Jesus our Lord" (Romans 6:23).

Defying Death

My performances and stunts are often referred to as "death defying." The fact is, I have only *avoided* death—so far. Jesus Christ, on the other hand, actually died, was buried, and on the third day rose again. By His resurrection He *defeated* death, so that those who put their trust in Him need never fear death again. The reality that Christ rose from the dead is absolutely essential for our salvation; in fact, the Scriptures tell us, "If Christ is not risen, your faith is futile; you are still in your sins!" (1 Corinthians 15:17). Since this issue is so important, how can we be sure that Jesus actually did rise from the dead—and that we can entrust our life to this Parachute?

Despite what many people believe, Christianity does not require a blind leap of faith. Instead, God has given us "many infallible proofs" of the resurrection (Acts 1:3), one of which is eyewitness testimony. After Jesus rose from the dead He remained on earth for forty days (Acts 1:3) instructing His followers, being seen by over five hundred people at one time (1 Corinthians 15:1–8), before finally ascending into Heaven (Acts 1:9–11).

Let's say each of those people who witnessed the resurrected Christ went to the witness stand and gave a 15-minute testimony of what they saw. If we began to hear their testimonies at 8 a.m. Monday morning, it would take all day, and all night, and Tuesday and Tuesday night, and all Wednesday, Thursday, and Friday. It would be late Saturday afternoon before they finished wrapping up their

The Perfect Parachute

testimony. It would take over 128 straight hours just to hear, for 15 minutes each, the testimony of every person who saw Jesus alive after He arose.

According to Dr. Simon Greenleaf, a founder of Harvard Law School, the resurrection of Jesus Christ from the dead is one of the most well-attested events of history, based on the laws of legal evidence used in court. In fact, Greenleaf was so convinced by the overwhelming evidence that he committed his life to Christ!

Through the resurrection of Jesus Christ we can have the promise of eternal life with Him in Heaven. We too can be raised from the dead to life, for Jesus conquered and abolished death for us all (2 Timothy 1:10). Just as He became our scapegoat and experienced our punishment to spare us, we are invited to experience His victory that we may live. Jesus said, "I am the resurrection and the life. He who believes in Me, though he may die, he shall live. And whoever lives and believes in Me shall never die. Do you believe this?" (John 11:25,26).

> *My performances and stunts are often referred to as "death defying." The fact is, I have only avoided death—so far.*

Putting on the Parachute

In addition to being set free from the shackles of sin through repentance, there is a second step required to complete our escape plan. We must accomplish both or we're still doomed. To stop the freefall we are in, we need a parachute—a proven, verified, trustworthy parachute. Jesus, the Son of God, is that Parachute. He is the only way to escape death. Jesus said, "*I am the way*, the truth, and the life. No one comes to the Father except through Me" (John 14:6, emphasis

ESCAPE OR DIE

added). He alone can land us safely on the other side of death.

Believing in parachutes, having a family member who wears one now and then, or even owning a parachute will not help you. You have to put it on for yourself. The Bible tells us to "put on the Lord Jesus Christ" (Romans 13:14). To "put on" in this instance means to place your complete trust in what Jesus alone did to save you. No human effort, good works, penance, church attendance, or charitable giving will impress God. Only Jesus Christ was worthy and paid the debt for us all.

I cannot emphasize enough that both of these steps must be done together and are essential for our salvation. We must exercise both "repentance toward God and faith toward our Lord Jesus Christ" (Acts 20:21). When you take those steps—repent of your sin and trust in Christ as your Savior and Lord—you become sinless in God's sight. Your shackles fall off and God's Parachute opens. Because Jesus destroyed the power of death, He is able to "release those who through fear of death were all their lifetime subject to bondage" (Hebrews 2:14,15). And Scripture assures us, if the Son makes you free, you will be free indeed (John 8:36)!

As a believer in Christ, you will have the assurance of eternal life in Heaven. Christ was condemned on your behalf, so it would now be "double jeopardy" for you to be tried for your sins; you can leave the courtroom exonerated. Your rap sheet was nailed to His cross and every sin you have ever committed will be removed from your record (Hebrews 8:12). No matter what you have done, or how unforgivable you think you are, God can forgive you through the cross of Christ.

When our records are wiped clean we are more than forgiven—we are justified. Think of that word as

The Perfect Parachute

meaning "just as if I'd never sinned." While it is true there may be earthly consequences we need to face because of our sins, the sins themselves have been expunged from our record and forgotten by God (Hebrews 10:17). In the same way that our sin was transferred onto Christ, His righteousness (right standing with God) is transferred to us (2 Corinthians 5:21). This is the holiness that is required to meet God's standard (Hebrews 12:14), so God sees us as holy or right in His sight. Therein lies the precious, inexhaustible power of the cross!

When you understand the depth of your sin, and realize what Jesus endured on the cross to save you from it, you will begin to understand God's great love. I am so grateful God chose to redeem us!

The High Wire

One time, while preparing for a particularly harrowing stunt, I noticed a spectator who seemed unusually interested in what I was doing to get ready. He explained to me that he had known the great tightrope walker Karl Wallenda and had often watched Mr. Wallenda set up his aerial rigging. This man continued by saying he admired such performances and that my intense attention to detail had reminded him of this circus legend he had met so many years before. Whenever I think of that kind compliment, it also brings to mind this effective illustration.

A high-wire artist had a cable stretched across Niagara Falls. Spectators watched in awe as he walked the wire, high above the churning foam of the mighty falls. As an added element of danger the performer pushed a steel wheelbarrow ahead of him to the praises of those mesmerized by his daring. He repeated the feat several times before pausing and addressing the crowd: "Do you believe I can do

ESCAPE OR DIE

this again?" Naturally, everyone thought he could, so he added, "Then who will get in the wheelbarrow?"

Many people say they "believe" in Jesus, but they have not truly trusted Him by putting their entire life into His hands. My own father sat in a church for twenty years and appeared to be religious, yet he was never really a Christian. Although he adhered intellectually to certain facts, he was not saved. It wasn't until he became seriously ill that he repented of his sin and placed his faith in Christ.

Faith has corresponding actions. You need to act on it. Just as the spectators were invited to exercise their faith in the performer by getting in the wheelbarrow, you are now invited to place your faith in Jesus. The Scriptures say, "Behold, now is the accepted time; behold, now is the day of salvation" (2 Corinthians 6:2). Put your trust in Jesus Christ today, as you would trust in a parachute to save you from sure death.

The greatest tragedy in life is not to fail in business or never see your dreams come true. It's not neglecting to get a college degree or disappointing your family's expectations. It's not even breaking our country's laws and going to prison for life. The greatest tragedy of all is to go to Hell for eternity because you consciously ignored all the warnings. You have the clear evidence of nature that there is a Creator. You have evidence in the daily news that men are evil and there is something seriously wrong with our world. You have the evidence from your conscience that you are guilty of breaking God's moral Laws. You now have the evidence from Scripture that Jesus, the Son of God, is the only one who can rescue you. If you choose to disregard these warnings, you will die and pay a debt in Hell that has already been paid for you 2,000 years ago. Don't be too proud to humble yourself before God and gratefully receive

The Perfect Parachute

His gift of eternal life. That would be the greatest tragedy of all. I beg you not to let that happen.

Pulling the Ripcord

Now that you know what to do, you need to do it. No one can do it for you. We often mistakenly over-complicate the gospel message. It was God who made it simple (2 Corinthians 11:3).

In conclusion, there are two things you need to do to be saved. You need to repent (turn from your sin) and put your faith in Jesus Christ. Your sin and Christ are polar opposites. When you intentionally turn from sin to Christ in simple faith, you will find that He will empower you to leave the sin behind. Talking to a preacher, going to the altar, reciting a rote prayer, or raising your hand during a church "invitation" can't save you. Joining a church, getting baptized, and taking communion are equally unable to save—as are all good deeds and religious works. No amount of expert arm flapping will enable you to overcome the law of gravity, and the Law of God is even harsher. Without a parachute, you will perish. Repenting and trusting Jesus Christ to save you is the only way to be released from the shackles of sin and escape death. It's God's way.

> *No amount of expert arm flapping will enable you to overcome the law of gravity. Without a parachute, you will perish.*

When you do that, you will have this wonderful promise from God: "Those who sat in darkness and in the shadow of death, bound in affliction and irons—because they rebelled against the words of God,... they cried out to the Lord in their trouble, and He saved them out of their distresses. He brought them out of darkness and the shadow of death, and broke their chains in pieces" (Psalm 107:10–14).

You can cry out to the Lord to save you right now. The moment you do, your sin record will be wiped clean and you will receive the gift of eternal life. This is one Parachute that is guaranteed to work every single time—without fail. It is God's will that we be confident of our salvation and secure in knowing that He who promised is faithful. Our assurance of salvation and the subsequent peace found in its guarantee is not due to an emotional experience or feeling, but is based on the bedrock of God's Word (Romans 8:16; 10:9; 1 John 5:13).

This great salvation is the experience that Jesus was explaining when He said that a man must be "born again" to see the kingdom of God (John 3:3). It is not logical to differentiate between a Christian and a "born-again" Christian. It would be like saying "a white Caucasian." There is no other kind of Christian than one who has been born again. When you repent and trust in Jesus, Christ comes to live within you through His Spirit. You are "born again" spiritually and become a member of God's family. You become an adopted child of God, and He becomes your heavenly Father.

At the beginning of this book I shared with you the following Scripture: "So teach us to number our days, that we may gain a heart of wisdom" (Psalm 90:12). We also discussed that wisdom is the application of knowledge. The Scriptures say that the fear of the Lord is the beginning of wisdom (Proverbs 9:10). Proper respect or fear of God is demonstrated by acting on His Word and heeding His warnings. You need to apply what you have read. Your destiny hinges on what you do with Jesus Christ. Two thousand years ago, the Roman governor Pontius Pilate asked a bloodthirsty mob what they would have him do with Jesus Christ. I ask you today, what will you do with Him? The Bible says we must choose today who we will serve (Joshua 24:15). The world's graveyards are filled with those who laughed at the gospel's warning only to die and lift their eyes in torment in Hell (Luke 16:23). They passed through the door of death unprepared and God gave them justice. It is now too late for them. It is not too late for you. *Now* is the day of salvation (2 Corinthians 6:2). Can you see the foolish bargain of enjoying sin for a season in exchange for Hell forever? Are you ready to turn from your sin to the King of kings?

Speak to Him in your own words from your heart. He is waiting and has promised to receive you (John 6:37). There is no other escape from death and Hell. I know—because He saved and rescued me.

"Our God is a God who saves;
from the Sovereign LORD comes escape from death."
—PSALM 68:20 (NIV1984)

CHAPTER 8

TRACKING

*"Cause me to know the way in which I should walk,
for I lift up my soul to You."*
—PSALM 143:8

Skydivers have a sense of humor. The men I was privileged to have working with on my aerial box escape were no exception. They were extremely professional yet knew when a clever remark would ease the tension. In an effort to introduce some levity into an otherwise serious atmosphere, one of them attached a small plaque to the inside of the box door just prior to my jump. It read "Watch Your Step." Indeed, the step I took out of the falling box left me in freefall at 6,500 feet. Christians who have been set free by Jesus Christ need to watch their step too. If you have become a follower of Jesus by putting your trust in Him, the Bible says you are to walk as He walked (1 John 2:6). As we look to God for His wisdom, we will learn to walk safely and not stumble (Proverbs 3:23).

When I escaped from the falling box, it was essential that I immediately get away from it. When a skydiver "tracks," he holds his body in such a way as to achieve some horizontal glide when falling. I had to learn how to do this or the box could have hit me when I opened my para-

ESCAPE OR DIE

Tracking away from obstacles

chute, and caused me great harm. When we are truly saved, God enables us to track away from our old life and those acts of rebellion that alienated us from Him and cause us great harm. That changed life is made possible through the work of God's Spirit, who now dwells within us. As believers, we are given a new heart with new desires and *want* to obey Him. We need to cooperate with God and go where the jet stream of His Spirit would lead us. This requires us to surrender our will to His. We are no longer the boss of our lives; He is. Scripture clearly says, "Do you not know that your body is the temple of the Holy Spirit who is in you, whom you have from God, and you are not your own? For you were bought at a price; therefore glorify God in your body and in your spirit, which are God's" (1 Corinthians 6:19,20).

I've taught Adult Sunday school for over a decade, and have had the privilege of both learning from and teaching others. The following sections contain principles that are the result of these experiences and of answering the

Tracking

questions of new Christians. If you are a believer, I hope you find the information useful as you learn to "watch your step" and "track away."

Expect Conflict

If you are a new Christian, make no mistake—conversion will bring conflict (John 15:18). Friends and family who have become accustomed to the chains they are wearing will question and perhaps even resent your newfound freedom (Matthew 10:36). You may be labeled a "Jesus freak," or people will think you've lost your mind over religion. Jesus gave us advance warning when He said, "'A servant is not greater than his master.' If they persecuted Me, they will also persecute you" (John 15:20). Sometimes the most difficult times are those right after our escape, as we begin to put distance between us and our old shackles. Friends you have perhaps known for years will criticize and wonder why you no longer participate in your old sinful lifestyle (1 Peter 4:4). Christians are still "in the world" but no longer participants in its value system (John 15:19). This can be a tough transition, but Jesus has promised us, "I am with you always, even to the end of the age" (Matthew 28:20). He has also set in place some principles that believers can put into practice to assist them in their walk with Him. Let's take a look at these principles and learn how to walk in true freedom.

Leap of Faith

I have jumped handcuffed out of perfectly good airplanes over a dozen times. It is often very difficult for other skydivers to film me because I'm falling so erratically. Generally speaking, I am falling back to earth and spinning, sometimes violently. In this position, speeds of 180 mph are attainable and subsequently the danger increases. My

ESCAPE OR DIE

Focusing on picking locks in freefall

attention is consumed completely on the task at hand: escaping from the handcuffs. I am thoroughly trusting that my altimeter is working correctly and I am not watching the ground. If my altimeter says 6,000 feet, then I believe that's what my altitude is. I have learned to trust it.

Most people would say that putting that level of trust in a mechanical device is both irresponsible and foolish. Those people forget that most of us trust our lives to mechanical devices every day. We trust that when we apply pressure to our brake pedal, our vehicle will stop. We trust that the seatbelt holding us securely will remain fastened and that the traffic lights telling us to stop or go will work correctly. This trust can also be called faith. The Bible explains faith this way: "Now faith is the substance of things hoped for, the evidence of things not seen" (Hebrews 11:1). Christianity is not a blind faith, but a confident assurance—based on the trustworthiness of God.

When I'm doing an aerial escape I don't need to see the ground to know how high up I am. I have my reli-

Tracking

able altimeter. In the same way, we can put our trust in God. In fact, the Bible says, "Without faith it is impossible to please God" (Hebrews 11:6). Unlike mechanical devices, God has a perfect track record for reliability and is ever faithful.

Some people believe mental assent is the same as faith. This is just a mental agreement that certain things are so, and it lacks corresponding action. Like the story I shared with you about my father, this type of "faith" is merely intellectual; it is never acted on. You may simply agree that parachutes work, but then instead of putting the parachute on you leave it under your seat in the airplane. In contrast, if you truly have faith that something is true, you will act on it. The Bible has the remedy to not only help us place our faith in God, but continue to increase our faith throughout our life: "So then faith comes by hearing, and hearing by the word of God" (Romans 10:17). The more we learn about our incredible Creator through reading His Word, the more we will trust our lives to His care.

Often, when student skydivers first learn to skydive, they tend to kick in freefall. Their legs grope around in the air trying to find some footing before they finally settle into a relaxed arch. In time, this behavior lessens until it stops altogether. We are all learning to more fully walk in faith. The kicking behaviors of worry and doubt can hinder the most seasoned of Christians. As we spend time with the Lord, we will find these hindrances will lessen in severity and duration.

Watery Graves

The press releases for my events often use the expression "watery grave," or say that I will attempt to escape my "would-be watery grave." That's an apt description of what is

ESCAPE or DIE

generally considered the Christian's first step of obedience to Christ: water baptism.

Water baptism is not magic and doesn't save anyone, and if applied to a nonbeliever will only produce a wet nonbeliever. Baptism is the means by which we identify with the death, burial, and resurrection of Jesus Christ. We are telling the world in a symbolic way that our old life is dead and buried with Christ, and we have been raised to live a new life (Romans 6:4), to serve the God of the second chance. Thank God for second chances!

It was the general practice in the early church to baptize new converts with water upon a profession of faith in Jesus Christ. If you have been born again, I would encourage you to be baptized at the earliest opportunity.

Flying the Pattern

Poet and musician Bob Dylan wrote in a popular song from the 1970s, "You're gonna have to serve somebody. Well, it may be the devil or it may be the Lord but you're gonna have to serve somebody." When the Christian has put on the perfect Parachute of Jesus Christ, he is not only saved from sin's horrible consequences, but he is freed from sin's mastery. The Bible tells us that we've been set free from sin, leading to death, and have become slaves or servants to God, leading to everlasting life (Romans 6:22). Few understood slavery better than America's sixteenth President, Abraham Lincoln. Nearly every day Lincoln would sit in the telegraph office during the American Civil War and get the latest tally of lives lost over the divisive topic. It's been said that when Lincoln told a young slave girl he had just purchased that he was setting her free, she asked, "To go anywhere I want to go?" Lincoln said, "Yes." The girl replied, "Then I'm going with you!" To serve a master who

Tracking

has purchased us out from under the bondage of sin and its horrific penalty is not hard. In fact, it is the true expression of gratitude that flows from a joyous heart. Yet, that servitude requires cooperation from us to be effective.

When a student skydiver is under an open parachute, he is coached into the landing area by radio. The instructor on the ground has the transmitter and the student has the receiver in a pocket sewn into the jumpsuit. The instructor is giving him commands, but the jumper, in order to fly the pattern indicated, still has to respond and cooperate with those commands. The student at no time becomes a mere robot in the instructor's hands. He can still ignore the instructor, drift out of the pattern, and get into trouble. Similarly, the apostle Paul encourages those who have put their faith in Christ to respond to God's direction as found in His Word and live the life that Christ has patterned for us.

As long as we are still in a physical body, the vestige of our old ways will want to steer us in the wrong direction. Sinful desires such as sexual immorality, anger, wrath, slander, and lying (Colossians 3:5–9) are just a few of the shackles that at one time mastered us. Having turned from them in repentance toward God, we have been empowered to replace them with the attributes of our new Master. Paul in the book of Romans instructs us to put to death those old tendencies and live lives according to God's direction. This is something that is premeditated and intentional and requires our obedience. Paul says to put on traits such as compassion, kindness, humility, meekness, patience, and forgiveness (Colossians 3:12,13).

If we follow God's pattern, we will keep ourselves from harm while at the same time being an effective representative of Christ to those around us. These Christlike qualities are often referred to as "fruit." They are attitudes and behaviors that are a result of having our hearts changed when we received Christ, yet require our cooperation in expression. This process is known as "sanctification" and is not an overnight phenomenon. In fact, the sanctification process is one that will continue throughout our life as we grow in our relationship with Jesus Christ. John Wesley said, "Every one, though born of God in an instant, yet undoubtedly grows by slow degrees." This growth is so important that Christians are encouraged to examine themselves to see if their lifestyles match their words (2 Corinthians 13:5). If there's no progressive change in your character, you need to ask yourself if you really turned to the Savior. No one who came to Jesus Christ was ever turned away (John 6:37), but no one who truly came to Jesus ever left the same person. If we truly possess what we profess (claim to have), it will be evident in our life (Matthew 7:16). Scripture teaches us that fullness of joy awaits those who obediently follow God's direction (John 15:11).

Treasure Hunting
Earlier I shared with you how a collection of handcuffs, locks, and restraints can be an invaluable reference tool for an escape artist. I need to qualify that statement. It is an invaluable reference tool for an escape artist *if* he knows how to use it and takes the time to study it. Over the years, I have met many people with handcuff collections, some of which eclipse my own. In having discussions with them I've noticed that the vast majority do not fully understand the mechanisms or how they work. Their collections just hang on the wall.

As a Christian you have a reference tool also; you just need to use it. Evangelist F. F. Bosworth is quoted as saying, "Most Christians feed their bodies three hot meals a

Tracking

day and their spirits one cold snack a week." The Scriptures reinforce the necessity of daily Bible study by saying, "As newborn babes, desire the pure milk of the Word, that you may grow thereby" (1 Peter 2:2). The Bible's sixty-six books are a truly invaluable collection, and if you study it, it will give you all the wisdom and knowledge you need for life—so you will be "complete" and "thoroughly equipped for every good work" (2 Timothy 3:16–18).

Sometimes people think that because my stunts and escapes are so daring, the things I do for personal recreation must be equally over the top. They imagine I must wrestle alligators, tame lions, or jump motorcycles for adventure and fun. Actually, the greatest adventures I've had have been spent with God and His Word.

One of the escapes I regularly perform is called "A Deadly Combination." In this challenge I am locked in a 350-pound steel safe from which I must release myself. Often we have a large video screen that displays the lock dial as it spins to dramatize my efforts to escape from the steel prison. As a locksmith and registered safe technician, I occasionally have the opportunity to open locked safes from the outside too. There is a great thrill in opening safes and discovering the secrets they contain. Safes were designed to keep people out, therefore, defeating them is a great way to sharpen a locksmith's skill. It's difficult to explain the exhilaration when the dial is turned for the last time and the lock finally opens.

On one occasion I opened an old Mosler fire safe that had been in a farmhouse basement for several decades. The original owners were long forgotten and the current owners were happy for me to take it off their hands. After working several weeks on the behemoth I was finally able to "crack" it without drilling any holes. When the safe door

ESCAPE OR DIE

finally swung open, I found myself looking at a virtual treasure trove of family history. Rifling through the papers I managed to find some names. I then had the pleasure of tracking down a middle-aged man and returning the documents to him and his family. Papers that had not seen the light of day for over fifty years, some dating back to the 1800s, were now in the hands of the rightful owner. Tears ran down his cheek as he held the historical papers—papers that were precious to him. In the same way, a thorough study of God's precious Word is an adventure that will not only increase your faith but give you the joy of discovering God's treasure trove of secrets and wisdom. I encourage you to read it, study it, and put it into practice. After all, if you're a child of God, it's your family history.

Cracking open an old Mosler fire safe

My ultimate goal for this book would be for you to know Jesus Christ as your Savior. Yet, if I only encouraged you to actually read the Bible for yourself, I'd say my efforts were not wasted. For in those pages, an honest soul truly seeking God will find Him. I have taken the liberty of including a "Bible in a Year" Reading Plan in the back of this book for your use.

Tracking

Guard Your Mind
Have you ever contemplated the fact that every action you ever committed began with a thought? That is why Scripture instructs us to control our thoughts so that they are pleasing to God and don't stray into areas that can injure us. It tells us to take every thought captive (2 Corinthians 10:5), because where we allow the mind to go, the body will eventually follow. I'd like to tell you a story from Scripture and give you an analogy of my own. These examples will help illustrate the importance of watching our thought lives.

Late one afternoon, David, the king of Israel, was walking on the roof of his palace. The palace roof gave David a bird's eye view of the surrounding buildings and the kingdom that God had entrusted to him. While meandering on the roof, David could see a beautiful woman bathing. David did some investigation and discovered that her name was Bathsheba and she was the wife of a man serving in his army. Despite the fact that she was married, David gave orders to have her brought to him. David took advantage of this opportunity; he committed adultery with the married woman and then sent her home.

That one night of sin was not without terrible consequences. Bathsheba sent word to David that their illicit one-night affair resulted in her becoming pregnant with his child. With her husband among those who had left the city and gone to battle, it would soon become painfully obvious to everyone that Bathsheba's pregnancy could not be attributed to her husband. David attempted several schemes to cover his tracks but none of them worked. He finally arranged to have Bathsheba's husband put onto the frontlines of battle where he was sure to be killed. That ruthless plot seemed in the short term to work. Bathsheba's husband was killed and his death attributed to the war—but in reality he was murdered.

King David, whom God called "a man after My own heart" (Acts 13:22), is often used as an example for us to emulate. This chain reaction of sin, however, is one of David's greatest failures and is recorded for us as a lesson—in hopes we will avoid similar pitfalls.

David was close to fifty years of age at the time of this incident. He had known God since his youth, and God Himself had appointed him as king over Israel. Yet, in a moment of weakness David was ensnared in escalating sin that resulted in another man's death. What he intended as an evening of forbidden pleasure led to murder. How could this happen? If this could happen to a man like David, how much more should we take care not to fall prey to the same type of failure?

For David (as for many of us), the problem began with the entertainment of what he saw. Now, notice I didn't say it began with what he saw—he couldn't control that initial glimpse—but by his entertaining thoughts about what he saw. David could not help the fact that Bathsheba was bathing at the moment that he happened to be on his roof. Yet he didn't have to continue to look and allow his imagination to produce imagery sufficient enough to compel him to send for her.

Note how the sin in this example continued to snowball producing ever-increasing sin. By allowing his thought life to get out of control, David became ensnared in an adulterous affair—with disastrous consequences. The Bible explains how this often deadly progression takes place: "But each one is tempted when he is drawn away by his own desires and enticed. Then, when desire has conceived, it gives birth to sin; and sin, when it is full-grown, brings forth death" (James 1:14,15).

The Scriptures tell us to avoid even the appearance of evil (1 Thessalonians 5:22, KJV) so as not to dishonor the Lord. In David's case, a "little look" led to murder. Fortunately, we can avoid similar snares by controlling what we think and meditate on: "Finally, brethren, whatever things are true, whatever things are noble, whatever things are just, whatever things are pure, whatever things are lovely, whatever things are of good report, if there is any virtue and if there is anything praiseworthy—meditate on these things" (Philippians 4:8). It's better to avoid temptation all together; yet, if it presents itself, God will give us the means by which to escape from it (1 Corinthians 10:13). We are to call on Him in the time of trouble (Psalm 50:15) and resist temptation with His help (Hebrews 2:18).

Often when I teach on this principle it strikes some people as extreme. After all, what is the harm in looking? If the example we just covered isn't enough to convince you of the potential danger, I often further illustrate it with the following story.

Prisons and Pythons

Song of Solomon 2:15 says, "Catch us the foxes, the little foxes that spoil the vines, for our vines have tender grapes." This verse points out that it is the "little" foxes that spoil the vines. The little pet sins we tolerate that are seemingly harmless can be devastating and deadly. Harry Ironside, former pastor of Moody Bible Church, in his commentary on the Song of Solomon alerts us to some of these "foxes": vanity, pride, envy, and evil speaking are just a few of the examples he mentions. He goes on to warn us about the dangers of neglecting to read the Bible, pray, and have fellow-

ESCAPE OR DIE

ship with other Christians. We don't tend to think of attitudes as sins, but these thoughts of the heart are what lead us to wrong actions. As we grow through God's Word, we become more sensitive in identifying these traits and more diligent in abandoning them. It will also make our conscience a more reliable indicator of right and wrong.

I used to do an act in which I was handcuffed and locked in a bag with an African python. The act was so well received that I was invited to perform it on Dick Clark's national television show in the late 1980s. "Live! Dick Clark Presents" was a variety show that gathered performers from a wide range of show business disciplines. It was there that I met Chubby Checker, Mackenzie Phillips, and other notables in preparation for my own appearance on the show.

The python used in this escape is not poisonous and is only about five feet long. When I opened for comedian Henny Youngman, he told me to get rid of the snake because it scared people. That's all I needed to hear. Perfect—that's exactly what I'm trying to do! The snake, of course, stayed in the act. One of the things an escape artist tries to do is face fears for people vicariously. The viewer is then invited to share the conquering of that fear and identify with the success of the escape artist. This is similar to the way people root for athletic teams and feel they share in their victories.

When doing this escape I always considered the snake a harmless prop, and for most practical purposes it was. I was invited to participate in a "DARE" anti-drug program in Deerfield, Illinois, one summer. As part of the promotion I was to escape from one of the holding cells at the local police station. In an effort to create more drama and interest in the event, the police and I decided that I would attempt the cell escape by first being handcuffed and

Tracking

locked in the bag with the python. Reporters from Chicago came to cover the event and the local media was buzzing over what I intended to do with this strange combination of cell and snake. The attempt began, as jailbreaks usually do, with a police officer conducting a complete search of my person from head to toe. I was then placed in handcuffs and leg irons before being led down a long, dark corridor to one of the empty cells in the jail. Following what had now become a well-rehearsed routine, I entered the bag and my lifelong friend Jeff Hansen wound the writhing python around my neck. I ducked down inside the bag while those on the outside locked the mouth of the bag shut. I heard the cell door slam shut and the footsteps of the media and police representatives fade as they left the cell block.

> *A five-foot python is with you—wrapped around your neck. As long as you're handcuffed... there's nothing you can do about it.*

Imagine for a moment: there you are, handcuffed in a bag and locked in a cold, dingy prison cell. You have been left entirely alone so no one can hear you cry for help. Yet you're not alone; a five-foot python is with you —wrapped around your neck. You can feel its muscular body slithering on you in the darkness. You know that as long as you're handcuffed... there's nothing you can do about it. It could strangle you, or it could just bite you; you are completely helpless. That's where I was.

So far, I'm thinking, *No problem*. But thinking "no problem" *was* the problem. I had done the bag escape many times before, except this time I was distracted because the handcuffs were unusual and I was locked in a cell. I ignored the snake because I had already deemed it as harmless. My time in the bag was spent concentrating on the hand-

ESCAPE OR DIE

cuffs, oblivious to what the snake was doing. After I had escaped from the handcuffs I looked up at the mouth of the bag. There is normally a small gap even when tightly closed that allows me to work on the exterior lock that holds the bag shut. This time, my heart sank: the snake was jammed in that gap in its own effort to escape! I then began what was to be a serious toe-to-tail wrestling match with a five-foot python (which is solid muscle) to dislodge it from the hole. I was lucky to win that fight. Without that gap, I would have remained a prisoner. By not taking that snake seriously I almost failed to escape from that jail. But the moment I had control of the snake, the rest of the escape went textbook. I'm grateful that the snake, unlike sin, didn't grow any larger the longer I shared my bag with it.

> Virtually all cobra envenomations if left untreated end in respiratory failure and a one-way trip to the morgue.

Skydiving instructors will tell you it is rarely the student skydiver who gets hurt. It is usually the expert who becomes complacent who makes the tragic mistake. Now, you may never wrestle with snakes or jump from planes, but you will have to guard your mind—yes, even from the "little" things.

After salvation, Christians will still not be perfect. Christ's right standing (righteousness) with God the Father has been credited to our account, yet we continue to grow in expressing that rightness in our actions. Our lifestyle of sin has changed, but as long as we are in the world we will wrestle with temptation. At times, we may fail both God and ourselves. God has made provision for that too. First John 1:9 tells us, "If we confess our sins, He is faithful and just to forgive us our sins and to cleanse us from all unrighteousness."

Tracking

The Arch Enemy

About ten years ago, pythons and boa constrictors just lost their appeal to me. It seemed too many people had them as pets and the fear that they aroused was not what it used to be. That's why I created "Live Cargo."

In this predicament I am locked in a cargo box that resembles (for those who remember) an old-fashioned phone booth. The box has a small, clear reptile cage bolted to its top. This clear cage is bottomless and mates with a hole cut in the top of the cargo box. The only thing separating this tiny enclosure from the box I'm in is a trap door, which is held shut by a short, taught cord. A hissing, five-foot Pakistani cobra is loaded into this enclosure in preparation for the challenge. I usually have an opaque bag placed over my head and manacles on my wrists before entering the box. Once I'm locked inside, the cord holding the trapdoor shut is set to break by a heating element. The object is to escape before the running brook of horror joins me in the cargo box. So far I have always escaped in time.

The cobra that is used in this escape is kept in a secure laboratory cage located in my basement studio. It was important that I study the behaviors of these reptiles before actually working with one in performance. This snake, unlike a python, is highly aggressive and stands at attention while flaring its signature "hood" whenever I walk by the cage. Strangely, my wife never goes in the basement. Whenever she needs me, she calls from the top of the stairs.

Cobra envenomation, unlike a bite from a nonpoisonous python, is extremely serious. The cobra's fangs are an effective delivery system for the snake's deadly neurotoxins. Virtually all envenomations if left untreated end in respiratory failure and a one-way trip to the morgue.

ESCAPE OR DIE

Christians have joined in an ancient battle and have a very real arch enemy, mentioned briefly earlier in this book. The Bible compares him to a deadly serpent and we know him as the devil, or Satan. Satan is a fallen angel who chose to rebel against God because he wanted to be equal to God (Isaiah 14:13). He hates God, and he hates God's creation—especially man, made in God's image.

Both the Bible and Jesus confirm that Satan is real (John 8:44). Being aware of his existence is the first step of our defense. He is not a fairy tale or man's way of explaining evil in the world. Just as there is a personal God (not an impersonal "force"), there is a personal devil. While this serpent's bite is no longer deadly to the Christian, he is not powerless. Satan's strategy is to make us ineffective for God, through temptation and deception, and his primary weapon—his venom—is the art of the lie. Just as God's Word is truth (John 17:17), Satan's word is a lie. In fact, he is called "the father of lies" (John 8:44). As with fake straitjackets, Satan's falsehoods can be detected by comparing them to what is genuine. Spiritual lies when placed next to the certainty of Scripture are readily identified.

The devil, as well as the world system or culture, and our own flesh (physical desires), will continue to oppose us during our time on earth. I heard of one man who asked his pastor to pray for him that he'll never have any more trouble with temptation or the devil. The pastor replied, "Do you want me to pray for you to die? Because that's the only way to be completely removed from temptation." While we are not removed from Satan's influence, God has given us both a defense and an offense to deal with our enemy. Called the "armor of God," you can read about this protective equipment in Ephesians 6:10–18. The most powerful piece of this equipment is our offensive weapon:

Tracking

the Word of God. When Jesus was tempted by the devil, He effectively resisted by quoting God's Word—an example we are to emulate (Luke 4:1–13). The best way to defend against a lie is to be armed with the Truth.

In November 1978 I was just a small boy watching the evening news with my parents, yet the gruesome images I saw that night remain with me to this day. Over nine hundred people lay dead in Jonestown, Guyana, in a remote South American jungle. Many of the little bodies I saw were no bigger than mine at the time. The families had gone there thinking they were following God but found the devil instead. Their leader, Jim Jones, had led them into a web of false teaching that culminated in one of the largest mass suicides in history.

We can probably all call to mind tragic examples of religious leaders who have led their followers away from the true God. David Koresh, of the Branch Davidians in Waco, Texas, and Charles Manson, who at times actually claimed to be Jesus Christ, are just two of the more blatant examples that come to mind. All cults, without exception, either isolate their members from the Word of God or convince them that they alone are the source of truth. Don't be led astray. Get to know your Bible (Acts 17:11)!

Like any creature, a cobra requires care. On a stormy night a few years ago I began the routine act of cleaning the snake's cage. This requires me to use snake hooks to transfer the animal from one cage to another. The primary cage is then empty and ready for cleaning. This particular evening, just as I transferred the snake and closed the lid, the power went out in our home. My imagination ran wild. If the power had gone out just seconds before, that cobra would have been suspended on my hooks in complete darkness and in neither cage. You don't appreciate the light until it's gone. When dealing with our enemy, we need the light of God's Word (Psalm 119:130). When dealing with cobras, a simple flashlight will do.

The Line Tender

Among my many career mementos is a small rope still tied in a loop and covered with my DNA. Said another way, I have an old, bloody rope in my collection. I was tied with that rope by a fireman during a performance when I was yet a teenager. It took what seemed like an eternity for me to get out of that rope and was a great embarrassment. You see, modern audiences, unlike their vaudevillian counterparts, will not wait forty-five minutes for an escape artist to free himself. So the six minutes it took for me to escape from that rope was met with little compassion. It also cost me several layers of skin, as evidenced by my crimson signature still quite apparent in its fibers. That unpleasant experience occurred as part of my learning curve. Several mistakes were made that almost resulted in an escape failure. I am completely self-taught so there was no one to warn or direct me as I undertook and learned new escapes. Looking back, I am indeed fortunate nothing worse has happened over my many years in the "school of hard locks."

Fellowship with other Christians is not only a great way for "iron to sharpen iron" (Proverbs 27:17) but is a great source of accountability and discipleship. Older Christians are in a position to help teach and encourage those new to the faith so they can avoid being enrolled in the spiritual "school of hard locks." If you recall, sin is described in Scripture as bondage. When people have been imprisoned a long time, they tend to develop habits and customs that are shaped by their boundaries. The term that is used in the natural world for this phenomenon is "institutional-

Tracking

ized." We hear people say that so-and-so has been in jail so long that he has become institutionalized. I've seen this trait in people as well as animals that have spent their whole lives in captivity. When the cage door opens they're not always sure what to do. The Church is there to help new believers make this transition.

When I was a young boy I saw George Pal's 1953 movie *Houdini* for the first time. It was wonderfully filmed, had a great cast, and was a giant Hollywood production. In the movie Tony Curtis, playing Houdini, is shackled and locked in a box, and is about to be lowered underwater through a hole in the ice of the Detroit River. Before the box has a chance to be gently lowered, the chain breaks violently and the box plunges through the hole to the bottom of the freezing river. Everyone standing on the ice begins to panic and Janet Leigh, playing Houdini's wife, faints. Houdini is shown to escape from the box and try to surface—only to find he is trapped beneath the ice. In one of the most nerve-racking scenes in the film, Houdini is pictured swimming beneath the ice, against the current, frantically searching for the elusive hole. The escape artist was able (by divine intervention or Hollywood magic) to find small pockets of life-sustaining air trapped between the water and ice. He would then float on his back long enough to inhale those pockets of air before continuing his search for the opening.

As a young man researching this escape, I was disappointed to find that although Houdini did a water escape in Detroit, the river was not frozen. To add insult to injury, he wasn't in a box either. Unfortunately, many of the stories of Houdini's life are like a hole in your sock; they just keep getting bigger over time. Having seen the dramatic Hollywood version, I vowed that I needed to make that escape happen for real. The escape was just too cool (pun

ESCAPE OR DIE

intended) to be left undone. I had the privilege of doing two under-the-ice cage escapes—one for a private film maker and the other for my ABC Television Special, "Secrets of the World's Greatest Escape Artists."

The first time I did the escape was undoubtedly the scariest. Our location for this media event was to be our local water-filled quarry. The quarry location was chosen as a deliberate attempt to face my childhood fears. This quarry had claimed a number of lives over the years and was a place of dread for me and many others growing up in my hometown. My goal was to meet that fear head on and at the worst possible time: winter! A steel cage was fabricated from expanded (perforated) metal and a crane was found to do the dunking. We were ready!

The day of the stunt began with the sound of chainsaws breaking the early morning silence. A hole had to be cut in the ice to accommodate the cage now turned potential death trap. After the ice was scored by the spinning blades, the giant ice slab was slid beneath the ice that adjoined it, leaving only a gaping black hole. The quarry cliff provided the perfect staging area for the box and crane so we took advantage of this natural perch and started the cameras rolling. First, I entered the scene wearing a wetsuit and was helped into the box by assistants. The wintriness of the February air was evident as every exhaled breath was captured by the ever-present video cameras.

We found during early water experiments that the buoyancy of the wetsuit could cause some unnecessary problems. We compensated for that possibility by adding a weight belt that I clamped around my waist as several lengths of chain were brought forward by volunteers. One of the chains was wound around my wrists and locked in place by a brand new lock. The other, longer chain was locked to the

Tracking

inside of the cage door and dropped through the grate in the bottom of the box. I ducked down as the chain was pulled tight closing the cage lid. The free end of the chain was secured to the outside of the box, completing the preparation of what was to be this crane's most unusual cargo.

The command was given to go and I felt the crane slowly lift me. As I watched the snow move beneath me through the grate in the bottom of the box, I began hyperventilating in anticipation of the most frigid breath hold of my career.

Anthony being lowered under the ice

My hands worked quickly and I freed them from the chains while I was yet in transit. The box paused over the hole in the ice...then descended. Water began gushing violently through the holes in the metal. First it was at my ankles and knees. Then it rose to my waist. Finally its icy embrace met my chest as I took a final deep breath. The cold water felt like a punch when it hit my torso and it took great presence of mind to not lose my breath during its assault. My ears popped and pressure was building in my head as the

ESCAPE OR DIE

box sank. The cage walls rumbled while air continued to be replaced by the frigid water.

When I finally came to a stop I was ready to separate fact from fiction. Is such an escape—under these circumstances—actually possible? I began working on the lock that held the cage lid shut, knowing that every passing second would rob my fingers of their ability to serve me faithfully. Rays of light from the underwater cameras were welcome visitors as they penetrated the holes in the cage and aided my efforts to defeat the brand new padlock. After a minute or so of concentrated effort, the cylinder of the lock turned and opened, unlocking the lid of the cage. I pushed open the lid and looked straight up. Seeing the light from the hole, I grasped the cable that had lowered me under the ice. I dropped my weight belt and used the cable to guide me to the surface and another successful escape.

Breaking to the surface—free!

The fact I'm writing this should tell you that both ice escapes, though performed six years apart, were successful. I'm sorry to inform you, though, there is no air trapped between the ice and water. I checked both times.

In the course of preparing for this escape, I worked with professional scuba divers trained in ice diving. We had to use our own local divers to operate the underwater cameras because the production company couldn't find divers from California who were willing to do it. I guess they were too used to their creature comforts and warm water. The advantage of living in Wisconsin, at least for this escape, is that there is rarely a shortage of cold weather.

I learned that it was standard protocol to have a line around the waist of the diver to prevent him from getting lost under the ice. The diver responsible for holding the line above the ice is called a line tender. There had been cases where divers had gone beneath the ice without a tether, only to exhaust their air supply and perish searching for the hole. Being in a cage, I would not only be without oxygen but without the security of a line tender.

Fellowship with other Christians is like having that line tender—someone to keep an eye out for your well-being and pull you to safety if you need help. Believers are called not only to encourage and pray for one another but to hold each other accountable to live lives that glorify God. I praise God for the line tenders in my life, and I encourage you to be involved in a local Bible-believing church. By doing so, you can have a safety line wrapped securely around you, and you can tend one for somebody else.

Talking to Your Father

The primary way we hear from God is through the Bible, but God also wants to hear from us, and the way He hears from us is through prayer. As Christians, we have the honor of being able to approach God as our Father because of our position of right standing in Christ. We can come before Him boldly and with confidence, demonstrating a firm belief that what Jesus did truly made us right with God (Hebrews 4:16).

ESCAPE OR DIE

Prayer has been defined as a heart-to-heart talk with God. The thing I like best about prayer is that I can be transparent with God. He knows me better than I know myself. Consequently, He is my best friend. Even when I've failed miserably, it's comforting to know the Lord is always gracious and near to those who call on Him (Psalm 145:18).

Don't worry about your prayer being "perfect." Since God knows our hearts, it's not the words that matter. It is not lofty eloquence that moves mountains. God moves when we, in right relation with Him, submit our wills to His and cast our cares upon Him in simple childlike trust. God is not a genie who is forced to act by our "incantations" or manipulated by clever phrases. He is the God of the universe who is genuinely and lovingly concerned for both our eternal and temporal needs. Martin Luther said, "Prayer is not overcoming God's reluctance, but laying hold of His willingness."

The story is told about a man in the early 1800s who purchased a ticket to board a large steamship bound for Europe. He spent all that he had for the ticket and had no funds left over to purchase meals or other luxuries. These voyages took weeks, so the man was forced to ration the cheese and crackers he had brought with him over the many days of the journey. The weary traveler lost weight but was grateful for the provision he had and tried not to crave the good fortune of those who ate in the ship's fancy dining hall. Upon reaching his destination, the man shared with a fellow passenger how hard his journey had been and how good it was to be back on dry land. If he never saw another cracker again it would be too soon. "That's a shame," the other passenger replied. "You should have asked—your meals were free with the ship's ticket!"

Tracking

The importance of talking to God in prayer daily is often missed by the new believer. We settle for the crackers of the world while the fancy dining hall of Heaven is neglected. Prayer is best demonstrated to us by Jesus and the early church. If our Lord felt the need to pray frequently, how much more should we follow His example (Mark 1:35)? The Bible says we do not have because we do not ask (James 4:2). It also tells us if we ask anything according to God's will, He will give us what we ask for (1 John 5:14,15).

Through prayer, we can revere and worship God (Daniel 4:34,35), or simply ask Him (and thank Him) for our daily needs (Matthew 6:11). As we spend time in the treasure house of God's Word, His will becomes known to us, and these are the things we are to pray for. We will then have confidence in our prayer life because our prayers will be firmly based on scriptural precedent.

I like to walk my audiences through some of my escapes by tapping into their imaginations. One method I use is to ask them to try to hold their breath for the entire minute it takes for me to escape from a pair of handcuffs. This exercise helps them to experience what it might really be like to do a daring underwater escape. We all want someone to be able to relate to us and our challenges.

Jesus Christ—God in the flesh—can empathize with humanity because He became a man. He felt pain, got hungry, became tired, and even cried. He was in every way tested as we are yet He never sinned (Hebrews 4:14–16). This should be a great comfort to us as we pray. The Lord knows experientially the difficulties of life. Seek God in prayer first and you'll glorify Him who is able to do "exceedingly abundantly above all that we ask or think" (Ephesians 3:19).

CHAPTER 9

DOING THE IMPOSSIBLE

"When His disciples heard it, they were greatly astonished, saying, 'Who then can be saved?' But Jesus looked at them and said to them, 'With men this is impossible, but with God all things are possible.'"
—MATTHEW 19:25,26

Physicist Lord Kelvin, president of the Royal Society, was quoted in 1895 as saying, "Heavier-than-air flying machines are impossible." We all laugh at that, and yet must concede that some things actually are impossible. While it is true that science has found ways to enable us to cross boundaries that at one time were thought to be impossible to traverse, man has yet to remedy his societal woes. Murders, adulteries, thefts, and wars plague an earth in dire need of a "heart transplant." This heart transplant can only be performed by God Himself and is the consequence of faith in Jesus Christ.

The born-again experience is a supernatural work of God that works alongside the free will of man. Man cannot "will" to become a new creature in Christ anymore than a donkey can will to become a race horse. Neither is the born-again experience forced on anyone. The Word of God enables the sinner to see his true state and produce the fruit of repentance. The sinner yields to the Spirit's conviction, turns from his sin, and puts his faith in Jesus Christ. All this would be impossible without God first calling us through His Word (Romans 10:14).

God has given all believers the solemn privilege of being a part of this miracle called the new birth. In what is known as the Great Commission, Jesus has commissioned His followers to share the message of forgiveness, telling us to "go into all the world and preach the gospel to every creature" (Mark 16:15). Even angels have not been given this honor. It has been reserved for those redeemed by the Lord Jesus Christ.

Holding the Light

In former times, boys often grew up to practice their father's trade. A boy would watch his father, listen to instructions, and learn to follow his example. My dad, just like Jesus, was a carpenter. He could do anything with wood. His wooden animal figures and hand-carved signs were displayed in art museums and nationally recognized institutions. He was also one of those people who could fix most anything and was very handy to have around. I must unfortunately confess, as those who know me will attest, I have not inherited any of these useful characteristics.

Early in my career, the television program "That's Incredible!" approached me to do an underwater coffin escape. In preparation for this, my dad built the coffin that was to be used in the escape. However, several failed stunts by others on that show caused the show's lawyers to rethink the prospect of having a minor risk his life on national television, and that opportunity fell through. It wasn't

Doing the Impossible

until several years later that I actually used that coffin as I was lowered underwater in it to publicize one of my appearances. Whenever my dad worked on a project like this, I was given the task of holding the flashlight for him—a task I did with much self-importance. I remember this with fondness, realizing (in retrospect) it wasn't so much that he needed me, as he was allowing me to spend time with him and share in the work.

When we obey the command to share our faith, God gives us the privilege of shining the glorious light of the gospel in our dark world. He has sent us to those who don't know Him, to "open their eyes, in order to turn them from darkness to light, and from the power of Satan to God, that they may receive forgiveness of sins…" (Acts 26:17,18). He does the inner work, but allows us to spend time with Him and share in that work. In gratitude, we can go out and share the same light that brought us out of darkness when we were shackled and in the freefall of sin. As we shine the biblical truths on the lost, the Lord honors that effort by promising that His Word will accomplish His purposes.

The Scripture actually states that God is making His appeal for reconciliation to the world through us. When we encourage those who are His enemies (as we once were) to give up their rebellion and surrender to Him, we are His voice: "We are ambassadors for Christ, as though God were pleading through us: we implore you on Christ's behalf, be reconciled to God" (2 Corinthians 5:20). What a humbling and sobering thought! What an honor to be so used!

If you are a Christian, there's only one reason you are here and reading this book. The Lord has left you here as a witness. In fact, preacher Charles Spurgeon is quoted as saying, "Have you no wish for others to be saved? Then you are not saved yourself. Be sure of that." These are strong words from a no-nonsense preacher. These words challenge us to cultivate a true concern and compassion for those who don't know Jesus Christ as Savior and Lord. Their eternal destiny is at stake. If you are not a Christian, it's God's mercy that has left you here so that you can come to the knowledge of the truth (1 Timothy 2:4). He doesn't want you to perish, but is waiting patiently for you to come to repentance (2 Peter 3:9). My entire purpose in writing this book is to convince you to be reconciled to God so you can escape death. Once you've done that, you can join Him in showing others how to be set free.

False Evidence

Jesus Christ gave us marching orders before He ascended into Heaven: "that repentance and remission of sins should be preached in His name to all nations" (Luke 24:47). Yet many Christians don't obey this command, and the greatest hindrance they cite to sharing their faith in Christ, or witnessing, is fear. God, our Creator, knows how we're wired. That's why throughout the Old and New Testaments, whether God is giving instruction through a messenger or preparing us to act on His instructions, there is a common theme: "fear not." Fear is multifaceted and can exhibit itself in many different ways. As you might have guessed, I consider myself a bit of an expert on fear. I would like to relate some of the things I've learned about this very real obstacle and the natural and spiritual ways we can diffuse it. Understanding what you're feeling and why you're feeling it will help to empower you to face the emotion of fear.

We are all familiar with fear's various symptoms: breathlessness, sweating, nausea, feeling shaky, etc. Science tells us there are two innate or primal fears: heights and loud noises. (Ironically, both of these are present when skydiving.)

Doing the Impossible

Some of our other top fears include snakes, speaking in public, being closed in a small space, spiders and insects, needles, mice, and, of course, death.

As we begin to examine fear in witnessing, I would like to share with you an acronym that has helped me. Think of the word "FEAR" as standing for False Evidence Appearing Real. It will help you to keep fear in perspective as we study it and, more importantly, to face it as you witness.

The Cognition and Brain Sciences Unit at the Medical Research Council in England released some interesting data in 2011. Using spiders and an MRI machine, scientists discovered results that suggest fear affects cognition, or how we perceive things. This is important when we try to understand our fears. We really can make mountains out of mole hills. Perception is everything. If we train ourselves to look at what's casting the shadow instead of the shadow itself, it will help us to bring reasonableness to what we're feeling.

> *Think of the word "FEAR" as standing for False Evidence Appearing Real. It will help you to keep fear in perspective.*

There are, in the natural sense, two types of fear: tangible fear and intangible fear. Tangible fear is present when there actually is a man-eating lion in the room. Intangible fear is present when we contemplate, *What if a lion came into the room?* One is understandable, though not necessarily helpful, while the other is irrational.

The adrenaline triggered by tangible fear can be helpful should we have to run or fight (the "fight or flight" response), even though fear itself is an emotionally charged response to danger. On the other hand, being cautious in genuinely dangerous scenarios is a rational response that need not carry with it the baggage that an emotional response would. One is cerebral while the other is emotional. All the physical symptoms from our list associated with fear are emotional reactions that detract from our ability to think clearly and be effective.

Intangible fear is even worse. It robs us of our effectiveness but it does so through deception. There is no way to come to a resolution when strategizing solutions to "what if" scenarios. There is always another hypothetical threat that quickly replaces the one before it. In witnessing, this usually takes the form of "What if I forget what to say?" or "What if I don't have an answer to a question?" These fears are based on wanting the approval of men instead of God. None of these "threats" is even close to facing a man-eating lion or hitting the ground at 180 mph.

Fear in witnessing is primarily a selfish emotion. It is a subtle form of pride that is self-preserving; we're afraid of appearing foolish, or of being ridiculed or rejected. However, it's been said we would be far less concerned about what others think of us if we only realized how seldom they do. Compassion for others and zeal for God can transform our fear into function. In essence, we can trample our fears underfoot when we are continually aware of the fate of those who die in their sins and that the Lord has promised to always be with us (Matthew 28:20).

Buried Alive

When I did the television special for ABC entitled "Secrets of the World's Greatest Escape Artists," hosted by James Brolin, one of the escapes I suggested we do is "Buried Alive." Others have done versions of this but they always depended on trickery to avoid the weight of the earth. In fact, when Houdini attempted this feat and failed, he later wrote

Doing the Impossible

that "the weight of the earth is killing." Initially, my intention in developing the stunt was to depart from all the traditional water tank escapes that have become a cliché among escape artists. The producers loved the concept, so it was off to the Las Vegas Hilton, where the sand flows as free as the money, for another daring exploit.

My version of the "Buried Alive" escape, which I called "The Crystal Crypt," involves being shackled inside an upright casket that has a clear glass front. The top of this casket is locked shut with a padlock from the inside. The padlock is brand new and removed from its original factory packaging on the spot. This is done not only to prove the lock is real and unaltered, but to give me the assurance that it hasn't been sabotaged to defeat me. I then enter the crypt through the clear glass front, and it is locked from the outside as well. My job is to escape from the shackles around my wrists and unlock the interior lock to get out of the top of the box. All this while the crypt, like the bottom of a giant hourglass, rapidly fills with 2,000 pounds of desert sand.

The Crystal Crypt

During the experimentation phase, I found that the very thing that could keep me a prisoner could be used against itself to free me. Sand can support the body's weight, unlike water (unless you're Jesus or Peter; Matthew 14:29). I learned that as I lifted my feet, every gap I created inside the crypt quickly filled with sand. With great exertion, I was able to strain up and out of the box by pushing against the sand to raise my body. As soon as I went up an inch, sand filled the gap so I could gain another inch. Fear is like that too. I like to call this principle "incremental mastery." The very thing that threatens to stop you, when it is conquered, can raise you to the next level. Courage is not possible without fear. Just as the body without the spirit is dead or faith without action is dead, there would be no courage without fear. Courage is not the absence of fear but the ability to act despite it. By facing and overcoming your fears, the experience gained will boost your confidence for the next time fear strikes.

> *Fear, like desert sand, can either bury you or liberate you. It's your reaction to it that will make the determination.*

Fear, like desert sand, can either bury you or liberate you. It's your reaction to it that will make the determination. I encourage you to incrementally face your fear and watch as you rise above its stifling weight.

Contagious Courage

Roger Nelson was my skydiving trainer and friend. He was the most charismatic man I ever met and projected a confidence that was infectious. He was a pilot and world champion skydiver, well known throughout the skydiving community as an innovator and pacesetter. President Kennedy once said, "Things do not happen. Things are made to happen." Roger, by God's grace, made things happen and was a man who won people's confidence easily.

Doing the Impossible

Roger dabbled with Christianity for many years before finally surrendering his life to Christ. A series of bad choices earned him a five-year prison stay, where he was forced to be alone with God. One of his cellmates during that stay ironically was a defrocked televangelist who continued to teach the Bible while in prison. The former televangelist encouraged Roger's study of the Word and Roger proved to be a source of comfort for him as he dealt with a painful divorce. I met Roger just prior to his stay in prison and we became reacquainted after he was released. He was to become one of my best friends.

Roger and I talked of the Lord often. I remember sitting in the cockpit next to him as we commented on the beauty of the cloud formations and the wonder of God. Roger confided in me and I slowly began to see the fruits of true repentance evident in his life. We were to start a ministry together and had planned to do a major outreach for the summer of 2003. Just two weeks prior to that outreach, my friend and brother in Christ, Roger Warren Nelson—like his brother before him—was killed skydiving. He and another jumper had a canopy collision less than 100 feet from the ground. Roger did not die instantly

Anthony and Roger practicing an airplane exit

but spent his last minutes on earth telling those who were trying to save his life about his trust in Jesus Christ.

Evangelist Billy Graham said, "Courage is contagious. When a brave man takes a stand, the spines of others are often stiffened." Confidence and fear are both infectious. When the Israelites sent out spies to investigate the land that God had promised to give them (Numbers 13–14), only two brought back a good report. Joshua and Caleb were confident that God would enable them to take possession of it. The rest saw only obstacles and dangers, and their fear infected all of the people, resulting in them missing out on God's best. Roger's courage was contagious, and he gave me the confidence to skydive. Prospective soul winners need to seek out fellow Christians who fearlessly share their faith. You'll find their fearlessness to be infectious, and soon you'll be the one others are seeking out for encouragement.

Soul winners also need to persevere. Vince Lombardi, former coach of the Green Bay Packers, is quoted as saying, "Once you learn to quit, it becomes a habit." The two hardest things I've done so far in my life were to preach my dad's funeral and to follow through with the outreach Roger and I had planned, without him. It was hard, but I had to do it. We are never promised that life would be easy —in fact, we are told we'll have trouble (John 16:33)—but we have to look ahead to the finish line. God will give you the grace to do what you need to do, often right before you need it.

My latest skydiving escape was done with Roger's son, Matthew (who was also involved in the canyon jump). Matthew, known as "Rook" to his friends, was just a child when I did my first jumps in 1988. I've seen a photo of father and son jumping tandem together when Rook was only six years old! When I see that picture, I like to look at

Rook's face. He's at peace. He's strapped to Daddy—and there's no fear. God has promised to give us His peace and has told us not to be troubled or afraid (John 14:27). Scripture also tells us not to fear man, and that if we trust in God He will keep us safe (Proverbs 29:25). We need to move forward and take Him at His unfailing Word.

Facing the Monster

Before I did my first parachute jump, I learned everything I could about skydiving. Before I purchased a python to share my bag with, I learned all I could about pythons. Before being submerged under the ice in a locked box, I learned all I could about the effects of cold water on the body. Our own minds create most of the scary monsters we face when dealing with fear. When we study and learn about the things we fear, it strips them of their mysterious trappings and they're left like the diminutive Wizard of Oz who tells Dorothy, "Ignore the man behind the curtain." Our monsters are then found to be mere illusions. (Remember, FEAR is False Evidence Appearing Real.)

The Bible not only commands us to share our faith, but it enables us to do so. Because God is just, He will never ask us to do something that He will not equip us to do. As we study God's Word, we will learn important principles to use in witnessing, including the necessity of repentance and the use of the Law to bring the knowledge of sin. In recent years author Ray Comfort has reinforced this most necessary principle to a church that has largely failed to use it. In addition, there are many excellent tools available that will educate believers and teach them how to share their faith. These resources are available from a variety of different sources. Many of the tools I like to use personally can be found at www.livingwaters.com. Living Waters supplies believers with materials to train and equip them to reach the lost effectively and, most importantly, biblically. Learning how to share your faith biblically will help to reduce your "fear factor."

However, if you're a Christian, you already know enough to share the gospel. The gospel message is remarkably simple: people are sinners and need to repent and trust the Savior. Scripture is filled with examples of people who, after being impacted by Jesus, immediately shared what great things God had done for them. These people weren't seminary graduates and had no PhDs; they had simply encountered Jesus Christ. The woman at the well in Samaria (John chapter 4) was not a learned religious leader, yet immediately after meeting Jesus she witnessed to her whole town, and many of the townspeople believed in Him because of her words. Start where you are and God will honor your obedience.

Don't let a lack of knowledge hinder you. Rarely does witnessing require an answer to a complex spiritual question. When it does and you know the answer, explain it. If you don't know the answer, be honest and say so. You'd be surprised how much people respect an honest answer. I often tell people, when I'm asked a question that I can't answer, that they should have asked me when I was fifteen years old and knew everything. As your knowledge grows, the day will come when you'll be able to answer some of the tough questions too.

Leaving the Step

I remember talking to a seasoned skydiver who used to comfort fearful people by saying, "You'll be fine once you leave the step." He was talking about the step of the airplane. Soul winning, like anything else, can be learned

Doing the Impossible

—but then the knowledge must be turned into action. At one time a lady criticized D. L. Moody for his methods of evangelism. Moody replied, "I agree with you. I don't like the way I do it either. Tell me, how do you do it?" The woman said, "I don't do it." Moody quickly responded, "Then I like my way of doing it better than your way of not doing it."

The local church is the grassroots expression of the love of God. It is the hands and feet of Christ reaching out to the lost. When I help local churches by using my talents as an escape artist, I am assisting in that work. Event evangelism is the means by which those who would normally have no interest in the gospel can be attracted to a venue where it will be preached. God used others to help me see how I could use my talents to do that. I suspect He will do the same for you. You can share your faith, powerfully and effectively, but you have to start.

> *I often tell people, when I'm asked a question I can't answer, that they should have asked when I was fifteen and knew everything.*

Former Chaplain of the U.S. Senate Peter Marshall said, "Small deeds done are better than great deeds planned." I didn't start skydiving in chains. I began with an instructor. Just like anyone else I had to learn one step at a time. One of the best ways to leave the step as a soul winner is to begin by using gospel tracts. Gospel tracts are printed cards or small brochures that present the gospel message. They take many different forms (even simulating money) and have the advantage, unlike a conversation, of lingering on coffee tables or automobile dashboards long after initial contact is made with people. According to the American Tract Society, 53 percent of all who come to Christ worldwide come through the use of printed gospel literature.

ESCAPE or DIE

Gospel tracts really are powerful. A friend of mine was saved after he had found a torn gospel tract in a restaurant bathroom as a teenager. The words brought conviction to his heart and were instrumental in bringing him to God. Some Christians don't think gospel tracts are effective, but the very thing that is despised and deemed worthless by some is the power of God to salvation for others.

To start out, you can simply leave gospel tracts in conspicuous places, so no human contact is required. Then you can hand them out to people with a friendly "hello" or "good morning." Before long, your comfort level will rise and you'll be able to approach people you've never met before and carry on conversations. None of this is possible, however, if you don't leave the step. So, start small and you'll be surprised how God can use you.

While I prefer doing escapes exclusively and have been called a purist, Houdini was both a magician and an escape artist. Often, he would blend the two disciplines together during his presentations. One of his acts was called "Metamorphosis." The trick involved Houdini being locked and tied in a trunk by his wife and then making a lightning quick exchange with her (behind a curtained enclosure) as she stood outside the box. Magicians still do the illusion and have brought the exchange time down to mere seconds.

The word *metamorphosis* is from a Greek word meaning "transformation" or "to be transformed." We usually think of the natural process of a caterpillar changing to a butterfly when we hear this word. The idea of transformation makes me think of the new birth, where we become "a new creation" in Christ (2 Corinthians 5:17). When I think of it in terms of witnessing, the apostle Peter comes to mind.

The Scriptures tell us that Peter was afraid after Jesus was arrested, and he denied the Lord three times as

Doing the Impossible

Jesus was on His way to the cross. Peter wept bitterly afterward (Matthew 26:75). Yet, after he received power by the Holy Spirit, this same timid, fearful man was transformed into a bold, nonstop evangelist. Peter, like most of the apostles, would lose his life for testifying to the gospel of Jesus Christ. In fact, tradition tells us that Peter was crucified upside down, by request, because he felt unworthy to die the same way as the Lord.

That same empowerment available to Peter is available to you. The Spirit who enabled Peter to be a fearless witness will do the same for you. You need to ask Him for boldness, then act on it. The apostle Paul said, "Pray also for me, that whenever I open my mouth, words may be given me so that I will fearlessly make known the mystery of the gospel, for which I am an ambassador in chains. Pray that I may declare it fearlessly, as I should" (Ephesians 6:19,20, NIV1984). Paul is asking for prayer so that he can declare the gospel without fear. If you are fearful, you are not alone; you are in very good company with Paul. We need to pray for one another that we would have boldness. We already know it's God's will that you and I witness, therefore we know He'll grant that request (1 John 5:14,15). The proper response for us, then, is to pray for it and go do it, believing He will give us the ability we need when we need it.

Just Do It

I enjoy stunt performers and always have. In a sense they seem like real-life superheroes. They appear to be impervious to the frailties that plague most of us and dare to do things that we can only dream of doing. Teddy Roosevelt spoke of those who "dare greatly," and pointed out how they, unlike the spectator, are actually in the "arena." They are not playing armchair quarterback and criticizing

ESCAPE OR DIE

how the strong man stumbled. They are actively engaged in the action. John F. Kennedy, when speaking of challenges and the motivation to meet them, said we choose to do these things "not because they are easy, but because they are hard." When I watch a world-record motorcycle jumper fly over 300 feet on his bike, or a high-wire artist tempt fate on a thin wire, it inspires me to think. It inspires me to think they're crazy! That's because I have not been desensitized to the same fears they have. These performers have practiced these stunts many times and have become accustomed to the various environments involved. They have developed unique skill sets that enable them to be successful in accomplishing their daring feats.

> *You don't want to waste valuable seconds; every 5 seconds, ten people die and enter eternity.*

Overcoming the fear of sharing our faith is as simple as practicing. Practicing desensitizes us to the things we fear. To remain "current" in their skills, skydivers try to jump frequently. When there are long gaps between jumps, some of those old fears can creep back in. I practice most of my stunts to the point that I can hardly stand to do them anymore. I can do them blindfolded, backwards, and falling from a plane! When actual practice is impossible, I like to use visualization. I've noticed skydivers doing this on the plane ride to altitude, actually going through hand motions and subtle body shifts mimicking their freefall maneuvers. Before I go witnessing or out to preach, I will pray first and then go through the mental exercise of rehearsing what I will say and the order in which I will say it. When you master this ability, it is possible to make even the most unfamiliar task a well-executed routine. Notice I said *pray first.*

Doing the Impossible

The fears that accompany witnessing are some of the most unreasonable fears there are, yet they are powerful. Don't underestimate the spiritual forces involved here. Satan is a real enemy to both God and man. This proud fallen angel and enemy of our souls will try to produce unreasonable fears to prevent us from sharing the Truth. Always remember to pray first.

If we make sharing the gospel a "practice," rightly defined as making something a habit or custom, our efforts will become more automatic. When skydivers prepare, they rehearse their emergency procedures until the required actions become instinctive. To have to think about a series of moves wastes valuable seconds, and every 5 seconds is another thousand feet. If you're always armed with the gospel and ready to share your faith, it won't be long until your witnessing actions will be automatic too. And you don't want to waste valuable seconds; every 5 seconds, ten people die and enter eternity—most ending up in the chasm of Hell. In skydiving and in soul winning, seconds count. So make it a practice. You can be a superhero for the kingdom of God!

Unbound

I've spent most of the years of my life studying the history and methods of the great escape. Behind every escape is the will to survive. Within these pages I've shared with you those things necessary for your survival. We've seen how God's Word is our escape plan that helps us to "number our days" by recognizing the freefall of our own mortality. We've also seen how the light of God's Law exposes our shackles of sin and warns us of God's coming judgment and the punishment of Hell. I have urged you to turn from the shackles of sin to the perfect Parachute of Jesus Christ —the only means possible to land us safely on the

ESCAPE OR DIE

other side of death. I've further emphasized the sense of urgency you should have in putting on this Parachute, if you haven't already, and to "cling to Him, for He is your life and the length of your days" (Deuteronomy 30:20). You now have everything you need to take that leap of faith.

Once you're under the open Parachute of God's love in Jesus Christ, you become enabled to go where the jet stream of His Spirit guides you. One of the clear goals of that guidance will be to empower you to share with others how they too can defeat death once and for all. You have in your hand the key to making the greatest escape. God has graciously done His part; now it's up to you to apply what you have learned and tell others about Jesus.

Without Him, there is no escape. With Him, the sky is the limit.

I hope to see you land safely on the other side.

CAREER HIGHLIGHTS

SEPTEMBER 13, 2011
Anthony is featured in the Ripley's Believe It Or Not! 2012 Annual.

AUGUST 22, 2011
Anthony returns to the Waushara County Jail 25 years to the day to duplicate his escape of 1986. He is strapped to a ladder in a straitjacket and locked behind 4 steel doors. He escapes in 2 minutes and 50 seconds, having again defeated the jail that held Edward Gein, "America's Most Bizarre Murderer."

JULY 12, 2011
Anthony films the first point-of-view video of an aerial handcuff escape while plummeting to the earth from 13,500 feet.

JUNE 13, 2009
Anthony is restrained in a chain configuration of 12 handcuffs that includes a 20-pound ball and chain. He is then locked in a cell at the Porter County Jail. He appears free in 8 minutes and 13 seconds having defeated the handcuffs and three locked jail doors to reach freedom.

ESCAPE OR DIE

OCTOBER 4, 2008
Anthony is searched and bound in an unaltered high-security straitjacket. All straps of the restraint were utilized including the side and belly loops. He was then locked in a cell of the Vernon County Jail. He escaped in 3 minutes and 10 seconds.

MAY 9, 2001
Creates "Live Cargo," an escape that incorporates the use of a cobra—one of the world's most dangerous animals.

JUNE 21, 2000
The Snake River Canyon, untested since Evel Knievel's attempt to tame it in 1974, is the location for Anthony's latest aerial "Dance with Death." Wearing handcuffs supplied by the Jerome County Commissioner's office, Anthony leaps from an airplane at 11,000 feet over the perilous gorge. He escapes in freefall, deploying his parachute and landing on the north rim having conquered the canyon.

NOVEMBER 1998
Launches Ambassador In Chains Ministries using the art of escape to proclaim the gospel of Jesus Christ.

Career Highlights

JANUARY 20, 1996
Anthony is featured in his first network television special. ABC airs "Secrets of the World's Greatest Escape Artists," which telecast the escapist's successful attempts to duplicate three of his most daring feats. The show concluded with Anthony's dramatic escape from beneath 2,000 pounds of sand at the Las Vegas Hilton in Las Vegas, Nevada.

AUGUST 6, 1994
Anthony leaps from an aircraft at 13,000 feet heavily chained and manacled. He successfully escapes in freefall, deploying his parachute and saving his life.

FEBRUARY 26, 1990
Anthony's hands are chained and he is locked within a metal cage with locks removed on the spot from their factory packaging. The cage was then lowered through a hole cut in the ice of a water-filled quarry. He escapes his watery tomb in 1 minute 45 seconds, becoming the first person in the world to perform an escape under the ice.

OCTOBER 12, 1988
The Los Angeles Police Department secures Anthony in a canvas bag with a five-foot African python. The bag is padlocked from the

ESCAPE OR DIE

outside with a lock removed from its original package by television celebrity Dick Clark. Anthony easily escapes in 20 seconds in front of a national audience of millions on "Dick Clark Presents."

SEPTEMBER 1988
Successfully executes an escape from a challenge pair of handcuffs within seconds in impromptu style on "The Late Show" with Ross Shafer.

AUGUST 28, 1988
Anthony is searched, restrained with two pairs of handcuffs, each covered in a black box and padlocked with locks sealed in their original packages (a black box is a device designed to cover and prevent tampering with the handcuff keyholes). He was then secured and chained to the interior of a freight box in which he was equipped with only a parachute. The box, having been designed with a jail cell lock, was itself locked and loaded aboard a cargo plane. Shoved out of the cargo bay at 13,500 feet and traveling at a terminal velocity of 130 miles an hour, Anthony escapes at approximately 6,500 feet and parachuted safely to the ground and into the record books, having completed the "Greatest Escape of All Time."

OCTOBER 31, 1987
Escapes in 2 minutes from the cell that held "Baby Face Nelson" at the Kewaunee County Jail in Wisconsin, after being restrained in leg irons and trussed in two straitjackets.

JULY 12, 1987
Escapes from the "Crystal Crypt," a box-like device that encased the performer behind thick plate glass while being buried in 2,000 pounds of sand.

Career Highlights

AUGUST 22, 1986
Earns the title of "King of Escapists" in Ripley's Believe It Or Not! after releasing himself from six sets of handcuffs and penetrating six prison doors at the Waushara County Jail in 4 minutes, 45 seconds. This is the same jail that housed Edward Gein, "America's Most Bizarre Murderer." The Gein case provided the basis for Alfred Hitchcock's movie *Psycho* and the films *Deranged* and *Texas Chainsaw Massacre*.

OCTOBER 17, 1984
Escapes from a police belly chain, handcuffs, and thumbcuffs after being locked in a U.S. Government mail pouch with a five-foot python coiled around his neck at the Pabst Theatre in Milwaukee, Wisconsin.

SEPTEMBER 24, 1984
Escapes after being bound in 20 pounds of chains secured with six padlocks, and confined inside a coffin. The coffin was tied twice at both ends with heavy rope, weighted at four points with burlap bags containing 500 pounds of rocks, and submerged in over six feet of water in the Sheboygan River, Wisconsin.

FEBRUARY 24, 1983
Videotaped escaping from a maximum-security isolation jail cell after being searched and restrained in eight pairs of handcuffs, a set of thumbcuffs, a belly chain, a leather restraining belt, and leg irons.

AUGUST 7, 1982
Over 2,000 people witness Anthony escaping from a locked, water-filled barrel after being submerged for over 3 minutes.

ESCAPE OR DIE

JUNE 16, 1980
Escapes from police belly chain, straitjacket, and maximum-security jail cell while appearing on the nationally syndicated television program "PM Magazine."

OCTOBER 26, 1979
Escapes from regulation police belly chain while appearing on the television show "Kids' World."

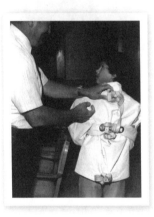

JULY 6, 1979
Escapes from handcuffs and straitjacket at Sheboygan County Jail, Wisconsin, after being searched and restrained by the sheriff.

DECEMBER 1978
At age 12, becomes youngest person in the world known to escape from a regulation police straitjacket.

AUGUST 8, 1976
First professional performance in Kiel, Wisconsin.

MARCH 15, 1976
Successfully executes first escape from regulation police handcuffs at age 10.

"Bible in a Year" Reading Plan

By investing about fifteen minutes a day, reading an average of three chapters per sitting, you will be able to explore all the treaures of God's Word in one year.

	Date	Today's Scripture Reading		Date	Today's Scripture Reading
☐	Jan. 1	Genesis 1–3	☐	Jan. 19	Exodus 7–9
☐	Jan. 2	Genesis 4–6	☐	Jan. 20	Exodus 10–12
☐	Jan. 3	Genesis 7–9	☐	Jan. 21	Exodus 13–15
☐	Jan. 4	Genesis 10–12	☐	Jan. 22	Exodus 16–18
☐	Jan. 5	Genesis 13–15	☐	Jan. 23	Exodus 19–21
☐	Jan. 6	Genesis 16–18	☐	Jan. 24	Exodus 22–24
☐	Jan. 7	Genesis 19–21	☐	Jan. 25	Exodus 25–27
☐	Jan. 8	Genesis 22–24	☐	Jan. 26	Exodus 28–30
☐	Jan. 9	Genesis 25–27	☐	Jan. 27	Exodus 31–33
☐	Jan. 10	Genesis 28–30	☐	Jan. 28	Exodus 34–36
☐	Jan. 11	Genesis 31–33	☐	Jan. 29	Exodus 37–40
☐	Jan. 12	Genesis 34–36	☐	Jan. 30	Leviticus 1–3
☐	Jan. 13	Genesis 37–39	☐	Jan. 31	Leviticus 4–6
☐	Jan. 14	Genesis 40–42	☐	Feb. 1	Leviticus 7–9
☐	Jan. 15	Genesis 43–46	☐	Feb. 2	Leviticus 10–12
☐	Jan. 16	Genesis 47–50	☐	Feb. 3	Leviticus 13–15
☐	Jan. 17	Exodus 1–3	☐	Feb. 4	Leviticus 16–18
☐	Jan. 18	Exodus 4–6	☐	Feb. 5	Leviticus 19–21

ESCAPE or DIE

Date	Today's Scripture Reading	Date	Today's Scripture Reading
☐ Feb. 6	Leviticus 22–24	☐ Mar. 11	Judges 1–3
☐ Feb. 7	Leviticus 25–27	☐ Mar. 12	Judges 4–6
☐ Feb. 8	Numbers 1–3	☐ Mar. 13	Judges 7–9
☐ Feb. 9	Numbers 4–6	☐ Mar. 14	Judges 10–12
☐ Feb. 10	Numbers 7–9	☐ Mar. 15	Judges 13–15
☐ Feb. 11	Numbers 10–12	☐ Mar. 16	Judges 16–18
☐ Feb. 12	Numbers 13–15	☐ Mar. 17	Judges 19–21
☐ Feb. 13	Numbers 16–18	☐ Mar. 18	Ruth 1–4
☐ Feb. 14	Numbers 19–21	☐ Mar. 19	1 Samuel 1–3
☐ Feb. 15	Numbers 22–24	☐ Mar. 20	1 Samuel 4–6
☐ Feb. 16	Numbers 25–27	☐ Mar. 21	1 Samuel 7–9
☐ Feb. 17	Numbers 28–30	☐ Mar. 22	1 Samuel 10–12
☐ Feb. 18	Numbers 31–33	☐ Mar. 23	1 Samuel 13–15
☐ Feb. 19	Numbers 34–36	☐ Mar. 24	1 Samuel 16–18
☐ Feb. 20	Deuteronomy 1–3	☐ Mar. 25	1 Samuel 19–21
☐ Feb. 21	Deuteronomy 4–6	☐ Mar. 26	1 Samuel 22–24
☐ Feb. 22	Deuteronomy 7–9	☐ Mar. 27	1 Samuel 25–27
☐ Feb. 23	Deuteronomy 10–12	☐ Mar. 28	1 Samuel 28–31
☐ Feb. 24	Deuteronomy 13–15	☐ Mar. 29	2 Samuel 1–3
☐ Feb. 25	Deuteronomy 16–18	☐ Mar. 30	2 Samuel 4–6
☐ Feb. 26	Deuteronomy 19–21	☐ Mar. 31	2 Samuel 7–9
☐ Feb. 27	Deuteronomy 22–24	☐ Apr. 1	2 Samuel 10–12
☐ Feb. 28	Deuteronomy 25–27	☐ Apr. 2	2 Samuel 13–15
☐ Mar. 1	Deuteronomy 28–30	☐ Apr. 3	2 Samuel 16–18
☐ Mar. 2	Deuteronomy 31–34	☐ Apr. 4	2 Samuel 19–21
☐ Mar. 3	Joshua 1–3	☐ Apr. 5	2 Samuel 22–24
☐ Mar. 4	Joshua 4–6	☐ Apr. 6	1 Kings 1–3
☐ Mar. 5	Joshua 7–9	☐ Apr. 7	1 Kings 4–6
☐ Mar. 6	Joshua 10–12	☐ Apr. 8	1 Kings 7–9
☐ Mar. 7	Joshua 13–15	☐ Apr. 9	1 Kings 10–12
☐ Mar. 8	Joshua 16–18	☐ Apr. 10	1 Kings 13–15
☐ Mar. 9	Joshua 19–21	☐ Apr. 11	1 Kings 16–18
☐ Mar. 10	Joshua 22–24	☐ Apr. 12	1 Kings 19–22

"Bible in a Year" Reading Plan

Date	Today's Scripture Reading	Date	Today's Scripture Reading
☐ Apr. 13	2 Kings 1–3	☐ May 16	Nehemiah 7–9
☐ Apr. 14	2 Kings 4–6	☐ May 17	Nehemiah 10–13
☐ Apr. 15	2 Kings 7–9	☐ May 18	Esther 1–3
☐ Apr. 16	2 Kings 10–12	☐ May 19	Esther 4–6
☐ Apr. 17	2 Kings 13–15	☐ May 20	Esther 7–10
☐ Apr. 18	2 Kings 16–18	☐ May 21	Job 1–3
☐ Apr. 19	2 Kings 19–21	☐ May 22	Job 4–6
☐ Apr. 20	2 Kings 22–25	☐ May 23	Job 7–9
☐ Apr. 21	1 Chronicles 1–6	☐ May 24	Job 10–12
☐ Apr. 22	1 Chronicles 7–9	☐ May 25	Job 13–15
☐ Apr. 23	1 Chronicles 10–12	☐ May 26	Job 16–18
☐ Apr. 24	1 Chronicles 13–15	☐ May 27	Job 19–21
☐ Apr. 25	1 Chronicles 16–18	☐ May 28	Job 22–24
☐ Apr. 26	1 Chronicles 19–21	☐ May 29	Job 25–27
☐ Apr. 27	1 Chronicles 22–25	☐ May 30	Job 28–30
☐ Apr. 28	1 Chronicles 26–29	☐ May 31	Job 31–33
☐ Apr. 29	2 Chronicles 1–3	☐ June 1	Job 34–36
☐ Apr. 30	2 Chronicles 4–6	☐ June 2	Job 37–39
☐ May 1	2 Chronicles 7–9	☐ June 3	Job 40–42
☐ May 2	2 Chronicles 10–12	☐ June 4	Psalms 1–5
☐ May 3	2 Chronicles 13–15	☐ June 5	Psalms 6–10
☐ May 4	2 Chronicles 16–18	☐ June 6	Psalms 11–15
☐ May 5	2 Chronicles 19–21	☐ June 7	Psalms 16–20
☐ May 6	2 Chronicles 22–24	☐ June 8	Psalms 21–25
☐ May 7	2 Chronicles 25–27	☐ June 9	Psalms 26–30
☐ May 8	2 Chronicles 28–30	☐ June 10	Psalms 31–35
☐ May 9	2 Chronicles 31–33	☐ June 11	Psalms 36–40
☐ May 10	2 Chronicles 34–36	☐ June 12	Psalms 41–45
☐ May 11	Ezra 1–3	☐ June 13	Psalms 46–50
☐ May 12	Ezra 4–6	☐ June 14	Psalms 51–55
☐ May 13	Ezra 7–10	☐ June 15	Psalms 56–60
☐ May 14	Nehemiah 1–3	☐ June 16	Psalms 61–65
☐ May 15	Nehemiah 4–6	☐ June 17	Psalms 66–70

ESCAPE OR DIE

Date	Today's Scripture Reading	Date	Today's Scripture Reading
☐ June 18	Psalms 71–75	☐ July 21	Isaiah 4–6
☐ June 19	Psalms 76–80	☐ July 22	Isaiah 7–9
☐ June 20	Psalms 81–85	☐ July 23	Isaiah 10–12
☐ June 21	Psalms 86–90	☐ July 24	Isaiah 13–15
☐ June 22	Psalms 91–95	☐ July 25	Isaiah 16–18
☐ June 23	Psalms 96–100	☐ July 26	Isaiah 19–21
☐ June 24	Psalms 101–105	☐ July 27	Isaiah 22–24
☐ June 25	Psalms 106–110	☐ July 28	Isaiah 25–27
☐ June 26	Psalms 111–115	☐ July 29	Isaiah 28–30
☐ June 27	Psalms 116–120	☐ July 30	Isaiah 31–33
☐ June 28	Psalms 121–125	☐ July 31	Isaiah 34–36
☐ June 29	Psalms 126–130	☐ Aug. 1	Isaiah 37–39
☐ June 30	Psalms 131–135	☐ Aug. 2	Isaiah 40–42
☐ July 1	Psalms 136–140	☐ Aug. 3	Isaiah 43–45
☐ July 2	Psalms 141–145	☐ Aug. 4	Isaiah 46–48
☐ July 3	Psalms 146–150	☐ Aug. 5	Isaiah 49–51
☐ July 4	Proverbs 1–3	☐ Aug. 6	Isaiah 52–54
☐ July 5	Proverbs 4–6	☐ Aug. 7	Isaiah 55–57
☐ July 6	Proverbs 7–9	☐ Aug. 8	Isaiah 58–60
☐ July 7	Proverbs 10–12	☐ Aug. 9	Isaiah 61–63
☐ July 8	Proverbs 13–15	☐ Aug. 10	Isaiah 64–66
☐ July 9	Proverbs 16–18	☐ Aug. 11	Jeremiah 1–3
☐ July 10	Proverbs 19–21	☐ Aug. 12	Jeremiah 4–6
☐ July 11	Proverbs 22–24	☐ Aug. 13	Jeremiah 7–9
☐ July 12	Proverbs 25–27	☐ Aug. 14	Jeremiah 10–12
☐ July 13	Proverbs 28–31	☐ Aug. 15	Jeremiah 13–15
☐ July 14	Ecclesiastes 1–3	☐ Aug. 16	Jeremiah 16–18
☐ July 15	Ecclesiastes 4–6	☐ Aug. 17	Jeremiah 19–21
☐ July 16	Ecclesiastes 7–9	☐ Aug. 18	Jeremiah 22–24
☐ July 17	Ecclesiastes 10–12	☐ Aug. 19	Jeremiah 25–27
☐ July 18	Song of Songs 1–4	☐ Aug. 20	Jeremiah 28–30
☐ July 19	Song of Songs 5–8	☐ Aug. 21	Jeremiah 31–33
☐ July 20	Isaiah 1–3	☐ Aug. 22	Jeremiah 34–36

"Bible in a Year" Reading Plan

Date	Today's Scripture Reading	Date	Today's Scripture Reading
☐ Aug. 23	Jeremiah 37–39	☐ Sept. 25	Amos 7–9
☐ Aug. 24	Jeremiah 40–42	☐ Sept. 26	Obadiah
☐ Aug. 25	Jeremiah 43–45	☐ Sept. 27	Jonah 1–4
☐ Aug. 26	Jeremiah 46–48	☐ Sept. 28	Micah 1–3
☐ Aug. 27	Jeremiah 49–52	☐ Sept. 29	Micah 4–7
☐ Aug. 28	Lamentations 1–3	☐ Sept. 30	Nahum 1–3
☐ Aug. 29	Lamentations 4–5	☐ Oct. 1	Habakkuk 1–3
☐ Aug. 30	Ezekiel 1–3	☐ Oct. 2	Zephaniah 1–3
☐ Aug. 31	Ezekiel 4–6	☐ Oct. 3	Haggai 1–2
☐ Sept. 1	Ezekiel 7–9	☐ Oct. 4	Zechariah 1–3
☐ Sept. 2	Ezekiel 10–12	☐ Oct. 5	Zechariah 4–6
☐ Sept. 3	Ezekiel 13–15	☐ Oct. 6	Zechariah 7–10
☐ Sept. 4	Ezekiel 16–18	☐ Oct. 7	Zechariah 11–14
☐ Sept. 5	Ezekiel 19–21	☐ Oct. 8	Malachi 1–2
☐ Sept. 6	Ezekiel 22–24	☐ Oct. 9	Malachi 3–4
☐ Sept. 7	Ezekiel 25–27	☐ Oct. 10	Matthew 1–3
☐ Sept. 8	Ezekiel 28–30	☐ Oct. 11	Matthew 4–6
☐ Sept. 9	Ezekiel 31–33	☐ Oct. 12	Matthew 7–9
☐ Sept. 10	Ezekiel 34–36	☐ Oct. 13	Matthew 10–12
☐ Sept. 11	Ezekiel 37–40	☐ Oct. 14	Matthew 13–15
☐ Sept. 12	Ezekiel 41–44	☐ Oct. 15	Matthew 16–18
☐ Sept. 13	Ezekiel 45–48	☐ Oct. 16	Matthew 19–21
☐ Sept. 14	Daniel 1–3	☐ Oct. 17	Matthew 22–24
☐ Sept. 15	Daniel 4–6	☐ Oct. 18	Matthew 25–28
☐ Sept. 16	Daniel 7–9	☐ Oct. 19	Mark 1–3
☐ Sept. 17	Daniel 10–12	☐ Oct. 20	Mark 4–6
☐ Sept. 18	Hosea 1–3	☐ Oct. 21	Mark 7–9
☐ Sept. 19	Hosea 4–6	☐ Oct. 22	Mark 10–12
☐ Sept. 20	Hosea 7–10	☐ Oct. 23	Mark 13–16
☐ Sept. 21	Hosea 11–14	☐ Oct. 24	Luke 1–3
☐ Sept. 22	Joel 1–3	☐ Oct. 25	Luke 4–6
☐ Sept. 23	Amos 1–3	☐ Oct. 26	Luke 7–9
☐ Sept. 24	Amos 4–6	☐ Oct. 27	Luke 10–12

ESCAPE OR DIE

Date	Today's Scripture Reading	Date	Today's Scripture Reading
☐ Oct. 28	Luke 13–15	☐ Nov. 30	2 Corinthians 10–13
☐ Oct. 29	Luke 16–18	☐ Dec. 1	Galatians 1–3
☐ Oct. 30	Luke 19–21	☐ Dec. 2	Galatians 4–6
☐ Oct. 31	Luke 22–24	☐ Dec. 3	Ephesians 1–3
☐ Nov. 1	John 1–3	☐ Dec. 4	Ephesians 4–6
☐ Nov. 2	John 4–6	☐ Dec. 5	Philippians 1–4
☐ Nov. 3	John 7–9	☐ Dec. 6	Colossians 1–4
☐ Nov. 4	John 10–12	☐ Dec. 7	1 Thessalonians 1–5
☐ Nov. 5	John 13–15	☐ Dec. 8	2 Thessalonians 1–3
☐ Nov. 6	John 16–18	☐ Dec. 9	1 Timothy 1–3
☐ Nov. 7	John 19–21	☐ Dec. 10	1 Timothy 4–6
☐ Nov. 8	Acts 1–3	☐ Dec. 11	2 Timothy 1–4
☐ Nov. 9	Acts 4–6	☐ Dec. 12	Titus 1–3
☐ Nov. 10	Acts 7–9	☐ Dec. 13	Philemon
☐ Nov. 11	Acts 10–12	☐ Dec. 14	Hebrews 1–3
☐ Nov. 12	Acts 13–15	☐ Dec. 15	Hebrews 4–6
☐ Nov. 13	Acts 16–18	☐ Dec. 16	Hebrews 7–9
☐ Nov. 14	Acts 19–21	☐ Dec. 17	Hebrews 10–13
☐ Nov. 15	Acts 22–24	☐ Dec. 18	James 1–3
☐ Nov. 16	Acts 25–28	☐ Dec. 19	James 4–5
☐ Nov. 17	Romans 1–3	☐ Dec. 20	1 Peter 1–5
☐ Nov. 18	Romans 4–6	☐ Dec. 21	2 Peter 1–3
☐ Nov. 19	Romans 7–9	☐ Dec. 22	1 John 1–3
☐ Nov. 20	Romans 10–12	☐ Dec. 23	1 John 4–5
☐ Nov. 21	Romans 13–16	☐ Dec. 24	2 John, 3 John, Jude
☐ Nov. 22	1 Corinthians 1–3	☐ Dec. 25	Revelation 1–3
☐ Nov. 23	1 Corinthians 4–6	☐ Dec. 26	Revelation 4–6
☐ Nov. 24	1 Corinthians 7–9	☐ Dec. 27	Revelation 7–9
☐ Nov. 25	1 Corinthians 10–12	☐ Dec. 28	Revelation 10–12
☐ Nov. 26	1 Corinthians 13–16	☐ Dec. 29	Revelation 13–15
☐ Nov. 27	2 Corinthians 1–3	☐ Dec. 30	Revelation 16–18
☐ Nov. 28	2 Corinthians 4–6	☐ Dec. 31	Revelation 19–22
☐ Nov. 29	2 Corinthians 7–9		

If you have put your trust in the
Perfect Parachute of Jesus Christ,
we'd love to hear from you.
For more details about
Ambassador In Chains Ministries,
or to contact Anthony Martin,
please visit our website:

www.anthonyescapes.com